PRACTICAL HERMENEUTICS

SCHOLARS PRESS
POLEBRIDGE BOOKS

edited by
Robert W. Funk

Number 1

PRACTICAL HERMENEUTICS
A Revised Agenda for the Ministry
Charles E. Winquist

PRACTICAL HERMENEUTICS
A Revised Agenda
for the Ministry

Charles E. Winquist

SCHOLARS PRESS

Distributed by
Scholars Press
101 Salem Street
Chico, CA 95926

PRACTICAL HERMENEUTICS
A Revised Agenda for the Ministry

Library of Congress Cataloging in Publication Data

Winquist, Charles E 1944–
    Practical hermeneutics.

    (Polebridge Books : no. 1)
    Includes bibliographical references.
    1. Clergy—Office. 2. Hermeneutics. 3.
Experience (Religion) 4. Psychology, Religious. 5.
Pastoral counseling—Case studies. I. Title.
BV660.2.W54   253   79-22848
ISBN 0-89130-363-4
ISBN 0-89130-364-2 pbk.

Printed in the United States of America
1 2 3 4 5
McNaughton & Gunn
Ann Arbor, Michigan 48106

For my father—

in appreciation for sharing his understanding of what is
real and important in the range of human experience

Part I

THEORIA

Chapter One

PRACTICAL HERMENEUTICS

The life of the church has been nourished by the theological self-consciousness of the clergy in expressions of parish life. The choice to lead through a commitment to serve is itself a symbolic announcement of the paradoxical vision of reality at the heart of Christian experience. The privilege and the cost of discipleship have been willingly accepted by generations of men and women in their response to a call to a life of ministry. This continuing resource has been a visible manifestation of the depth of religious life in the midst of historical change.

The many challenges to the vocation of the ministry in the life of the contemporary church threaten the possibility of Christian life and are not merely the displacement of individual clergy from traditional patterns of leadership. If we affirm the concept of a priesthood of all believers, the understanding of ministry should be a critical concern for any systematic expression of theology. The concept of the ministry cannot be determined in isolation from the problems that have challenged the viability of theology as a whole. Foundational questions that explore possibilities for religious discourse are profoundly significant in the definition of ministry.

Concepts of ministry are so closely allied with social institutions it is easy to lose sight of their theological meaning. Too often our understanding of service is little more than an ideological response to contemporary social problems. With a faltering self-consciousness the actualization of ministry can dangerously approach the simple imitation of fashionable secular solutions to human problems. The danger of this movement is not that social problems

1

lack urgency and significance; nor is it the fear that secular solutions are inadequate and lack depth. The danger is that these concepts of ministry are usually removed from the base of understanding in which the secular solution is grounded and also become forgetful of the religious experience at the root of conversion. I am not suggesting that the concept of ministry should be removed from the front line of social problems. I am concerned that we address ourselves to the right questions so that we can discern the locus of regenerative power in defining possibilities for a meaningful concept of the ministry. Our understanding must avoid narrow definition. The call to the ministry that encompasses the priesthood of all believers reaches beyond the vocational definitions of social work or psychological counseling, political or social movements, and intellectual or ideological currents. Certainly the historical embodiment of religious consciousness must be acknowledged, and it is clear that the full range of human experience confronts the concept of ministry with a challenge to be taken seriously. This is a recognition that the cost of discipleship can only be known in the middle of experience and that there can be no historically disembodied ministry. However, the relevance of religious consciousness cannot be ascertained by simply acknowledging that it is in the world. There is no other possibility. We must understand the function of ministry and then decide if that function is important.

Generalized definitions of the word *minister* suggest the notions of servant and attendant. In the secular usage of the word we can clearly define the particular meaning of a ministry by pointing to the object of its concern. The ministry of . . . is a ministry of defense or finance or any of the other many functions that are needed in the fulfillment of an institutional program. In each case the ministry of . . . is determined by the reality to which it attends. The translations between secular and religious concepts of ministry are ambiguous because we have not clearly defined the needs or realities to which we attend or serve. The structure of the ministry is clearly intentional, but the function of the ministry cannot be determined until we can identify the object of intentionality that gives religious significance to the concept of ministry.

There are many specific answers that readily can be given to the search for an intentional object of ministerial concern. Hunger, despair, injustice, and racism are all exemplary problems manifested in everyday life that are within the range of religious concern, but they are not uniquely religious problems. The inclusion of any specific area of human need into a statement of the function of the ministry relies on the validity and applicability of a more general definition for its meaning.[1] The concept of Christian ministry will be deficient in meaning until we can outline a general understanding of its function. If there is no general reference to the intentional structure of Christian ministry, we will not be able to build a unified foundational concept of the ministry that enfranchises specific statements with religious meaning.[2] The specific commitment to service is intertwined with a general transformation of consciousness, but too often we have lost the meaning of conversion in our definition of ministry. Conversion is the turning event that transforms the meaning of ministry from a secular to a religious concept. We confess that we have experienced a new reality: a reality to which we will attend in the definition of ministry. The concept of ministry is not an adjunct to theological understanding. It is the practical expression of a new consciousness, and the minister is an attendant to the intentional object of this new consciousness. Thus, the first object of our foundational inquiry into the ministry is the nature of religious experience.

Religious Experience

A doctrine of the ministry that is functionally defined in relationship to the concept of religious experience will always be subject to the moving edge of contemporary theological debate. The meaning of religious experience is never securely anchored in one theological system. Contemporary theology is in dialogue with the secular sciences, philosophy, and the history of religions. Basic concepts of reality and intelligibility function heuristically and are constantly subject to revision by the exigencies of experience.[3] Even the concept of religious experience is a methodological construction that must be judged by its explanatory power. This means that the idea of a unified foundational concept of the ministry is not invariant throughout different theological models.

---

[1]Cf. Stephen Toulmin, *Human Understanding: The Collective Use and Evolution of Concepts* (Princeton: Princeton University Press, 1972), p. 69.

[2]Foundational inquiry pursues transcendental questions concerning the possibility and underlying structure of experience. In modern philosophy the Kantian questions concerning the formal possibilities for objective knowledge have been extended to inquiry into the formal possibilities for experience itself. The search for foundations of experience is functionally equivalent to the quest for a beginning or origin of experience. The attraction of foundational inquiry is that it begins in the middle of real experience and always maintains this empirical reference. The search for foundations is a search for the forms or structures that are necessary for the reality of experience that is already present in consciousness.

[3]Concepts function heuristically when they anticipate the intelligibility of what can be known. They are provisional explorations into the meaning of experience.

The sense of reality that informs the concept of ministry will be different as we change theological perspectives. At first it appears that I am suggesting that the concept of ministry is to be set free in a sea of intellectual relativity. It is this possibility that has paralyzed many students of theology before the challenge of foundational inquiry. It is easier to remain on the surface of thought and experience than to plumb their foundations. It is, however, no less risky. The irony of a retreat to the surface is that the surface will crack when there is a shaking of the foundations.

In fact, I am suggesting that the concept of the ministry is to be anchored in the reality of experience. For example, when I see a pink elephant I can then say that I have seen a pink elephant whether that pink elephant is a private or collective phenomenon. The experience begs for explanation, and the simple recognition that systems of explanation are relative does not dislodge the primacy of experience. Even if we admit the possibilities of distortion and disguise in the presentation of experience to consciousness, this is a phenomenon that requires interpretation but is also a real fact of experience. The commitment to the immediacy of religious experience as the foundation for the development of our conceptual understanding stabilizes the religious meaning of a doctrine of the ministry. It may be that our religious experience is not profound and the subsequent development of a concept of the ministry is proportionately shallow. This can only be determined by an examination of religious experience. A profound concept of the ministry cannot be rescued from a shallow concept of religion.

A very inclusive definition of religion is simply the human response to moments of transcendence.[4] We have all experienced expressions of meaning that reach beyond the ordinary determinants of everyday life. Our dreams, our hopes, our visions, and even the flickering consciousness present in deep emotional relationships suggest meanings that transcend what we ordinarily mean by intelligibility and reality. Many people have claimed that they have had experiences that are wholly other from their ordinary experience, and almost all of us have experienced brief glimpses of meaning that cannot be fully articulated by familiar patterns of description and explanation. In both examples the salient characteristic of the experience is the presence, anticipation, or intimation of meanings that stretch the limits of secular models of intelligibility. If these experiences have sufficient density to be

---

[4]Charles E. Winquist, *The Communion of Possibility* (Chico, California: New Horizons Press, 1975), p. 67.

noticed and are close enough to conscious processes of self-realization, they alter our expectations for satisfaction and fulfillment in life. Although they seldom totally refute established patterns of meaning, religious experiences can displace the focus of our striving for meaning from the center of ordinary achievements. The need to discover a depth that does not disappoint the new expectations originating in a glimpse of transcendence becomes a central theme of religious life.

The desire to have our world turned upside down or to have consciousness transformed is a recurrent theme in modern culture. The disappointment with the surface of experience is so pronounced that it has even been productively exploited by modern advertising. We are all familiar with cosmetic, soft drink, and clothing commercials that associate their products with symbols of religious transformation. There are three examples that are so blatant that I think they deserve our attention. The first is a perfume commercial that portrays the ordinary rhythm of housekeeping and motherhood as drab but necessary. The perfume is then associated with a radical transformation that promises an evening of excitement and intimacy. The transformation is physical and mental. The lyrics of the song accompanying the visual images of physical transformation claim that during the day "I've been nice and I've been good" in contrast to the promise of the night. The second commercial for denim clothes is an animation of a sleepy street with dreary figures bent over with boredom. A messianic figure appears and transforms the sleepy street into a vibrant affirmation of life by miraculously dressing the figures in new denim clothes. The mysterious messiah leaves after the radical transformation of the community. The third commercial that attracted my attention was for a popular soft drink. On a rural hilltop a very integrated group of people are singing that "I want to teach the world to sing in perfect harmony." This utopian image of unity among the races, nations, sexes, and generations is punctuated by a massive soft drink bottle descending from the heavens. The lyric of the song changes and affirms that the soft drink is "the real thing." The ability to reach out and take hold of reality is thereby associatively connected with a vision of unity and the soft drink.

Disappointment with the surface of experience and the desire for transformation even reaches into the very heart of the marketplace. However, the desire to be turned around or upside down is also at the heart of religious experience. If we haven't experienced expressions of meaning that reach beyond the ordinary determinants of everyday life, we would like to have this experience: that is, we seek a conversion.

There is no single experience that can be offered as a paradigm for religious conversion. The turning around that is suggested by the notion of conversion will always be clothed with fabric of its historical particularity. We do note that in many illustrious conversion stories there is usually an element of paradox and surprise that defies simple imitation. The conversion experience that transformed Saul into Paul on the Damascus Road is certainly exemplary of a transformation that is contrary to our expectations as well as Saul's expectations. We have no reason to think that the vision of the resurrected Christ was willed. There is no formula for conversion that can be abstracted from this story. The recognition that where sin abounds grace much more abounds is the foundation for hope and not a model to be imitated in the search for a satisfying religious experience. The confession that grace exceeds sin is the fruit of a new consciousness. The origin of this new consciousness is the gratuitous and paradoxical interruption of the sacred into profane experience. The story of Saul's conversion to Paul is a dilemma for the righteous and diligent seeker of God. The concept of grace confounds the longing for perfection and opens up the possibility for faith.

Elie Wiesel tells a story from the life of the Maggid of Kozhenitz that illuminates the impossibility of imitating faith. A woman came to him because she wanted a child. The Maggid told her that his mother was also barren until she met the Baal Shem Tov and presented him with a cape. The woman happily responded by telling the Maggid that she would bring him a beautiful cape. He said that it would not help her. The difference was that his mother did not know this story.[5] The paradox of conversion is no easier to penetrate than the faith of Maggid's mother. There is no pedagogy for conversion or transformation. The call to commitment precedes the articulation of ministerial possibilities. The greatness of the gift of the cape to the Baal Shem Tov by the Maggid's mother was that it was gratuitous. It preceded knowledge of the story. The conversion of Paul preceded his ministry. He attended to the reality of his new consciousness and thereby shaped the meaning of his ministry. We know the story of Paul. It cannot be fruitfully imitated. There would be no paradox and no conversion.

Conforming to an established story is not the same thing as being turned around. If we omit the paradox of conversion from our concept of the ministry we should look carefully to see whether we have disguised the reality of our sin. We can even use the concept of sin as part of the disguise for the separation that

[5] Elie Wiesel, *Souls on Fire* (New York: Vintage Books, 1973), p. 132.

permeates our lives and constitutes the most profound experience of our sin. When we are too willing to confess our sinfulness, it is probably not *our* sin that we are confessing. Even conforming to the expectations of a religious community is not what is meant by conversion.

Sometimes the expectations of a religious community can be overturned by the conversion of an individual. Clifford Geertz tells the fascinating story of Kalidjaga's conversion to a Muslim without ever having been in a mosque, seen the Quran, or heard a prayer.[6] It is not only an individual's conversion story, but it is also a challenge to the traditional Muslim conception of the surrender to Allah. Kalidjaga became a Muslim because he was transformed. He did not reform because he became a Muslim. This story is of particular interest to our study because of the priority of the conversion experience and the secondary importance of belief. The paradox of the conversion experience can be clearly observed.

Before his conversion Sunan Kalidjaga was named Raden Djaka Sahid. He had an earned reputation for gambling, whoring, drinking, and stealing. According to the story, when Sunan Bonang, a Muslim, came to Djapara he was well-dressed, covered with expensive jewels and carried a solid gold cane. Raden Djaka Sahid confronted him and demanded his clothes, jewels, and cane. Sunan Bonang laughed and rebuked him for his pointless desire. Sunan Bonang then transformed a banyan tree into a tree of gold draped with jewels. Raden Djaka Sahid's expectations were radically overturned by recognizing that possessions of this world were nothing compared to the power of Sunan Bonang. The tale continues by telling how Raden Djaka Sahid was transformed into Sunan Kalidjaga by faithfully attending to the reality of his new vision. He was called to the service of a new consciousness that was radically different from his consciousness of puny objects of desire.

The story of Jesus' calling of Simon, James, and John in the Gospel of Luke (5:1–11) is not as elaborate as the story of Kalidjaga's conversion but it interestingly parallels it. While Jesus stood by the Lake of Gennesaret, he noticed two boats by the water's edge and fishermen washing their nets. Jesus told Simon to put his boat into the water and, after he finished speaking to the crowd that he had gathered, told Simon to let down his nets for a catch. Simon protested that they had fished all night and caught nothing, but he did let down his nets. The catch was so large that the nets began to split, he called for his friends, and both boats were loaded almost to the point of sinking. When Simon saw what had happened, he fell

---

[6]Clifford Geertz, *Islam Observed: Religious Development in Morocco and Indonesia* (Chicago: University of Chicago Press, 1971), pp. 27–29.

before Jesus. He was amazed and transformed by the power of his new consciousness from a fisherman into a fisher of men. He attended to the reality of his new vision by leaving everything and following Jesus. The story of the calling of Simon, James, and John is primarily a story of conversion. As their expectations were turned around they had a new vision. Their ministry was a commitment to serve and attend to this new consciousness of reality. The expectations of their old consciousness were fulfilled and transcended in their encounter with Jesus. Their old vocation was superseded by a new agenda for life.

It is perplexing to note the elliptical character of any description of the content of a conversion experience. In the two examples that I have cited, the revelation of new reality is embodied in a process of expectations and the turning around of those expectations. Certainly we cannot reduce the vision of Kalidjaga to a golden banyan tree or the vision of Simon, James, and John to a net full of fish. The concept of calling and conversion is dynamic and draws attention to the act of revelation. The act implies more than the specific content of revelation. In Christian theology the recent emphasis upon a word-event as distinct from word-content is an implicit reformulation of the concept of revelation that is closely related to the concept of conversion needed to understand the meaning and possibilities for the future of ministry.

Revelation

Revelation should be understood as an act or event in a foundational investigation. Certainly a content is dialectically related to the act, but it is the structure of the act that enables us to understand the congruency of conversion and revelation. We usually associate the idea of revelation with seeing or hearing rather than with our other senses, although revelation can also be identified with understanding. We are hearers of the word of God, and being hearers of the word of God opens to us a new vision. The image of seeing something new is closely related to the concept of conversion. When we turn around, we see differently. The horizon has shifted and the foreground of our vision is different. It is possible that we are re-collecting what we have seen before, but we are gathering this experience under a new horizon and from a different perspective. Few of us will have conversion experiences that are public dramas. However, what we see in our world can be profound and satisfying.

Revelation occurs because we are turned around by the promise of a more profound experience. As we turn around, our vision is expanded and our experience is altered by the new realities that enter our field of vision. Conversion is revelation because we see and know more than we did before we turned around. We all share a priestly function as we attend to the realities that we see. This is the primary meaning of ministry. Because we live in different worlds, the intentional content of revelation will be different for each of us. A golden banyan tree draped with jewels and a net full of fish do not exhaust the meaning of revelation. It is unlikely that any of us will have this content woven into a conversion experience. The focus of these stories is on the miracle of the conversion and not on the historically unique content of an initial image. Even when these images function symbolically, they do not constitute the miracle of conversion and the transformation of consciousness, although they can be constitutive elements in the act of transformation. We have been sensitized by Paul Ricoeur to the possibility that the symbol can give rise to thought.

The biblical reports of the conversion experiences of the early disciples of Jesus are too sketchy for us to know clearly what Jesus said with any certainty. We have a much clearer report of the "good news" that was taught by Jesus in his general ministry and in the teaching and preaching of the early church. The claim of Jesus that the kingdom of God has entered into history, as well as the church's confession that Jesus is the Christ and that he is risen from the grave, characterizes the content of the word of God that precipitates conversion. The message of Jesus is an invitation to celebrate the nearness of God in a fragmented world, and the proclamation of the church is a confirmation that this invitation continues to be meaningful beyond the cross. The proclamation of Jesus is a word of acceptance. Even though we have not merited living in the presence of the kingdom of God, it is here now. If we can accept our sin, and if we can accept that we are accepted even though we are sinners, the possibility is offered to us to re-collect our experience in a richly expanded world of new meanings. Carl Jung has said that the only thing that really matters is whether we are related to something infinite or not.[7] The importance of the word of acceptance in the preaching of Jesus is that it gives us permission to approach the "infinite" within the range of our experience. We do not need to hide from God because of our fear of judgment if we think that righteousness has been graciously imputed to us. The paradox in the proclamation of Jesus is that we are invited into the presence of God even though we are aware that the quality of our lives does not warrant such an invitation. It is not the invitation that is the revelation. The revelation occurs because we are able to

[7]Carl G. Jung, *Memories, Dreams, Reflections* (New York: Vintage Books Edition, 1965), p. 325.

discern the presence of an ultimate meaning through the re-collection of experience. A revelation occurs because the world is allowed to embody a meaning that has long been symbolized as an unknown God.

Before we can understand this notion of revelation we need to clarify the idea of a hidden God. The paradox of conversion can be appreciated only when we can see the word of acceptance in contrast to our natural expectations. The witness of generations is that there are manifestations of the sacred that interrupt the everyday world and also that the depth of the sacred is hidden and ineffable. There is a Muslim ritual that dramatizes this insight. With the counting of beads the names of Allah are cited. These names point to the wonderful presence of Allah in the world. When the Muslim comes to the one hundredth name, he/she confesses that Allah cannot be named. The wonderful presence of Allah is conjoined with the awful hiddenness of Allah. Wonder and awe are valuations of transcendence. Allah has been manifested into the world of experience but transcends and judges the adequacy of our posture before the reality of transcendence. Jewish scripture also witnesses to the unspeakable name of YHWH. It is almost at once obvious that an unconditional reality cannot be understood or explained in conditional categories. That is, it should be no sur-prise to us that God cannot be understood and that theological explanations must acknowledge incompleteness. Theological clo-sure is an intellectual failure. Theology can never transcend its fallibility without ceasing to be a human endeavor.

In spite of our intellectual inability to understand the reality of God, we still talk about God or the manifestation of ultimate reality within the confines of our experience. Carl Jung chiseled in stone above the door to his home in Kusnacht a quotation from Erasmus that "Called or not called, God will be there."[8] Even if we do not understand God, we are confronted with interpreting the meaning of the presence of God. For some of us the quote above Jung's door or the proclamation of Jesus that the kingdom of God is breaking into history is frightening rather than reassuring. The polarity between grace and judgment is evident in the ambivalent response to the announcement of the presence of God. Ultimate reality overwhelms a judgment on the worth of provisional human projects. We experience ourselves as inadequate before the claim that purity of heart is to will one thing. We back away from the graceful presence of God to avoid a judgment that shadows the dignity of human achievements. We deny ourselves the grace of

[8]This quotation is from the oracle at Delphi, as it is cited in the works of Erasmus.

God by choosing not to see ourselves against an unconditional horizon. The fallibility of the human condition is disguised in our escape from ultimate reality. This inability to see ultimate reality is a perversity rather than a fallibility of the intellect. That is, we choose against seeing the manifestations of God in the marketplace of experience because of our fear of judgment. God is hidden from secular consciousness because we are anxiously hiding from ourselves.

The ability to distort and disguise reality has been well documented in psychoanalytic thought.[9] Psychology provides an important clue to understanding the dynamics of revelation. Paul Tillich in *The Courage to Be* has defined neurosis as the affirmation of a partial self.[10] We avoid the threat of non-being by avoiding the fullness of being. We disguise and limit our vision of what it means to be human so that we do not approach the boundaries of experience where the fragile achievements of life are sometimes threatened. That is, we choose to narrow the neighborhood in which we live in order to remain in safe and familiar territory. Because we are finite we are vulnerable to death, the paralysis of guilt, and the loss of meaning. This vulnerability makes us anxious.

The thread of individual identity is buffeted by the winds of fate and will eventually be cut by the inexorable reality of death. We cannot reverse the givenness of life or death. We can, however, hide from the demands of both givens because they make us anxious. We can extract our lives from the terrible vision of transience if we are willing to sacrifice promise, hope, fidelity, care, and other complements of the human agenda that have a temporal determination. If we void the possibility for meaningful relationships, we can even escape the shock of everyone's death but our own. In the escape from the knowledge of death the self that is affirmed is reduced. In contrast the possibility for an affirmation of the whole self is a victory over death. St. Paul's claim that in Christ there is a victory over death is closely related to his insight that sin is the sting of death. His theology is not an escape from our fallibility. We remain standing before the reality of death, but death cannot extinguish the eternal that is visible in the presentation of the world under an ultimate horizon. If we hide from a confrontation with the unconditional and become separated from the depth dimension of our own existence, then death is a condition of judgment that abrogates the significance of any human projects. It is easy to see

---

[9]Cf. Paul Ricoeur, *Freud and Philosophy: An Essay on Interpretation* (New Haven: Yale University Press, 1970), p. 162.
[10]Paul Tillich, *The Courage to Be* (New Haven: Yale University Press, 1952), p. 66.
[11]*Ibid.*, pp. 40–42.

why we resist a knowledge of our finitude when it speaks of our death if we see no victory over death. We subsequently halt before the realization of possibilities that transport us into regions of experience that illuminate life on the border of death. We fear the natural rhythm of growing older because we have no myth that allows us to live into our death. It is not death but life that will be cheated by the failure to consent to our finitude. The resistance to self-understanding has its foundation in our inability to see a significance to life that reaches beyond the sentence of death. Choice is paralyzed by the relativity of finite values. This resistance to self-understanding and the denial of freedom are important concepts in exploring the meaning of revelation.

We have already acknowledged that revelation is an event and cannot be fully understood if we only examine the content that is reported in recording the event. The symbology present in the content of revelatory experiences can be distorted if it is disembodied from the fullness of the event. In fact, in many examples the symbology can be interpreted so that it illuminates the event quality of the revelatory experience. It is not unimportant that in the conversion story of Kalidjaga it was a tree that was transformed into gold and draped with jewels. His transformation of consciousness was a transformation of the world symbolized through the microcosm of the tree. The tree has traditionally served as a symbol of the cosmos, life, the center of the world, and support of the universe.[12] Revelation means the transformation of the world through the transformation of consciousness. The relationship between the symbol of the fish and the concept of the self has been examined by Carl Jung and suggests that there is archetypal significance to the transformation from a fisherman to a fisher of men in the calling of Peter, James, and John. This presence of *transformation* symbolism in conversion stories draws our attention to the act of transformation itself as the meaning of revelation.

It is consciousness that is transformed, and the possibility for that transformation is announced in the conversion story. The fact that consciousness is directed toward an object means that it is historical and worldly. When consciousness is transformed, the world is saturated with new meanings and described by new adjectives. Imagination generates new metaphors that anticipate the unity and intelligibility of this new world. We suddenly find ourselves in the age of Pisces or Aquarius. The kingdom of God is at hand. The warped and dreary actualities of everyday life appear fresh and harbor new hope.

---

[12]Mircea Eliade, *Patterns in Comparative Religion* (Cleveland: The World Publishing Co., 1963), pp. 266–67.

The symbolism of conversion is only the beginning. Mature religious consciousness develops beyond a conversion event through a growth of understanding nurtured by the positive symbolic content of revelation. The meaning of ministry is elucidated by the ongoing interpretation of meanings that accompany conversion. However, the nurturing of a new vision is secondary to that vision itself. The concepts of conversion and revelation can be obscured by examining only their secondary development. Theology is an interpretive endeavor that expands the vision of religious consciousness. It is usually secondary to the original constellation of events that constitutes the conversion experience. This does not preclude its possible role as a constitutive element in the origination of religious consciousness. In that instance theology has become proclamation and the secondary interpretive role follows. The revelatory event occurs when the remoteness of God becomes the nearness of God. Interpreting the meaning of the presence of God is therefore naturally secondary to the revelation itself.

The psychological dynamics of revelation and conversion are available to a first level of analysis. The notion of the hiddenness of God can be explored independent of specific theological presuppositions. It has already been acknowledged that we hide from a dimension of ultimacy in our experience because it judges the inadequacy of finite human projects. That is, the nearness of God is disguised by our choice. To avoid the anxiety of confronting our finitude we hide from a vision of transcendence that could establish a contrast that makes us conscious of our finitude. By denying this foundational contrast, consciousness dims and we see neither the self in its finite nakedness nor the presence of God clothed in unconditional judgment. We have temporarily escaped the anxiety of self-recognition. Ironically, we have also sacrificed the possibility for self-fulfillment. The sense of emptiness or meaninglessness that we sought to avoid slowly permeates everyday experience. We face a meaninglessness but, unlike the threat of meaninglessness, death, and guilt that accompanies self-understanding, this meaninglessness is mute and gives no clue to its power.

It is in the midst of the pathology of everyday experience that revelation announces the possibility for a new vision of the self and the world. In a gratuitous conspiracy of events it sometimes happens that the masks that disguise the presence of unconditional possibilities and judgment are removed. This may be an extraordinary experience similar to the conversion of Kalidjaga, or it may be a new juxtaposition of what had been ordinary events. The well-known parable of the mustard seed in Buddhist teachings illustrates what I mean by a new juxtaposition of ordinary events.[13] There is profound revelatory significance to the story of Kisa Gotami. Her son, whose birth was the basis for her respect in the community, died when he was just old enough to run and play. After failing to find a miraculous medicine to revive her dead son, she sought the wisdom of the Tathāgata. He saw that she was ready for conversion and sent her to every house in the city to collect the grain of a mustard seed to prepare a medicine from each of the houses that had never been touched by death. When she returned to the Tathāgata, she understood transience and inevitability of death. Her consciousness of what is real had been transformed by an extension of the meaning of finitude.

In the teachings of Jesus we see another possibility for turning consciousness around so that it can take account of its own finitude and no longer hide from the presence of ultimate meanings. Jesus preached that the kingdom of God is here. It is breaking into history even though it has not been earned by the faithfulness and righteousness of the people. This is a message of acceptance. In some ways it parallels the importance of the quote from Erasmus that "Called or not called, God will be there." The invitation to repent and participate in the kingdom of God expresses the nearness of God and is a message of acceptance. As Paul Tillich has suggested, you are accepted but you must accept the fact that you are accepted.[14] You must strip off the mask of righteousness used to disguise your fragility and finitude before you can enter into the kingdom of God that is here in spite of your unworthiness. To be conscious of ultimate reality present within historical experience you see yourself against the horizon of ultimacy. Thus, there are two expressions of acceptance in this concept of revelation. First, there is an acceptance by God in spite of our sinfulness. Second, there must be an acceptance of ourselves as sinners, which is made possible by the prior acceptance of us by God. We are able to look toward an unconditional reality and see ourselves as finite because we have been accepted into the power of that unconditional reality. The power to see ourselves is the same power that enables us to recognize dimensions of ultimacy that permeate our world. The graceful acceptance of the sinner gives us permission to come out from hiding and look freshly at the conditioned world as it appears against an ultimate horizon.

---

[13]E. A. Burtt, Ed., *The Teachings of the Compassionate Buddha* (New York: Mentor Books, New American Library, 1955), pp. 43–46.
[14]See Paul Tillich, *The Shaking of the Foundations* (New York: Charles Scribner's Sons, 1948), pp. 153–63.

The structure of revelation that can be recognized in religious consciousness is similar to the self-disclosure that can occur in a psychotherapeutic setting. In some therapeutic models you purchase acceptance either directly or indirectly. After being accepted for therapy you do not risk the harsh judgment of society if you reveal infantile aggression or eroticism. Societal repression is temporarily bracketed in the sanctuary of the consulting room. Thus, the therapeutic situation is an isolated possibility for the exploration of human feelings and thoughts that have been repressed or obscured by the flattening of experience in the adjustment to everyday life. The self is enlarged by admitting into consciousness feelings that are its natural possessions. More importantly the range of consciousness is extended by enlarging the base of relational patterns in the establishment of relevant contrasts for consciousness to reach out into new regions of experience. This increase in consciousness is the vitalization of possibilities. What was possible is brought within the effective range of the actualization of experience. It is not an exaggeration to speak of a new life and a new world when consciousness comes out of hiding.

The invitation and variations on the invitation to repent because the kingdom of God is entering into history is a magnification of the privileged psychotherapeutic situation. Repentance is actually made possible by the claim that the kingdom of God is at hand. The lifting of individual history into a context of ultimate significance is a valorization of the self that reaches beyond the determinants of our individual history. The self is not extinguished by the recognition of individual weaknesses and failures. That is, the acknowledgment of our finitude is not a resignation or capitulation to the threat of nothingness. The paradox that resides in the call to repentance is that consciousness of finite meanings is rooted in a contrast with the possibility for ultimate meaning. The dissatisfaction with the surface of experience can be thematized in conscious thought only when we relate to contrasting deeper levels of experience. It is the possibility for this deeper and more profound experience that allows us to admit that the surface of experience is not satisfactory. This consciousness is saturated with the possibilities for a deeper level of satisfaction. In this sense the gracefulness of possibility abrogates the terror of judgment.

The transformation of world-consciousness is a corollary to the transformation of self-consciousness. The power of the revelatory event is extended into the world. This is one expression of the intersection of the kingdom of God with the horizontal flow of human history. Every aspect of human history is implicated in the power of transformation because history is reinterpreted against the background of a deeper and more satisfying vision of reality. Social history becomes subject to prophetic judgment. The relativity of provisional goals is quickly ascertained when experience is viewed against an ultimate horizon.[15] The social gospel, theologies of liberation, and the individuality of pastoral counseling are all manifestations of the interpretive power of a new consciousness. Even if we have not chosen to change our perspective, the unveiling of a new horizon has in fact altered our perspective. The proclamation of Jesus forces a decision. An invitation is not an information item that can be catalogued or disposed. We either must accept or reject the invitation if we have been hearers of the word. If we reject the invitation, we are forced into the masking and disguise of our experience. Kisa Gotami had either to deny her experience of the reality of death or transform her consciousness of what is real after following the wisdom of the Tathāgata. Ministry that is grounded in revelation and conversion serves the vision of a new reality that permeates the full agenda of human life. Fresh patterns of meaning emerge from a deepened perception of external reality against the numinous background of an unconditional horizon.[16] Ministry comes to a fulfillment as it weaves these meanings throughout the fabric of everyday life.

Practical Hermeneutics

The importance of theoretical studies in hermeneutics for practical explorations of the ministry is the formation of new categories for understanding critical turning points in religious experience. Ministry is an interpretation and implementation of possibilities that are discerned at the heart of religious experience and can thus be understood as a practical hermeneutic. Interpretation can be *praxis* as well as *theoria*.

The concept of ministry is revised when it is aligned with a theological understanding of the word as event instead of the word as content. Without denying the specificity of the content of the word-event, the focus of interest is shifted to the interpretive power of the word from simple interpretation of the word. Legalism and

---

[15]We associate the visual image of the horizon with the farthest distance that we can see from any particular perspective. If we climb a mountain and our view is not obstructed, the horizon encompasses a larger field of vision. I use the image of an ultimate horizon to suggest the opening up of a field of unrestricted vision. In actual fact, the immediacy of experience remains a finite achievement, but the range of meaning that surrounds experience is not prematurely closed. The range of possibilities is unlimited and could only be encompassed by an ultimate horizon.

[16]Cf. Aniela Jaffé, *The Myth of Meaning* (New York: Penguin Books, 1975), p. 80.

literalism are recognized to be misappropriations of the functional significance of the word-event.

The primary meaning of ministry must incorporate conversion and the calling into the service of a deeper vision of reality. The transformation of consciousness is both a re-ordering of values and a new perception of meanings. New meanings and values influence action and judgment. The interpretive power of the word is practically implemented through everyday functioning in what has become an extraordinary world. The agenda for ministry evolves out of the situational presence of a new consciousness in the world of historical experience. There is no escape from the weight of history or the facticity of the objective world. A sacred mountain remains subject to physical forces and geological processes. The fact that it is sacred in a particular religious tradition does not extricate it from the nexus of relationships that constitute the meaning of its physical presence. In the same way the sanctification of history does not lift us above the tangle of political and economic forces within the secular history. Even apocalyptic metaphors are historically embodied in the signification of meaning if they have not become empty labels. Lifting personal and collective history into a context of ultimate meanings is not a denial of history. There is a similarity to Paul's proclamation of a victory over death not being a denial of the reality of death. Attending to the new reality received through the transformation of consciousness is a worldly enterprise.

There remains a necessity for theological reflection in this revision of the ministerial agenda. The transformation of consciousness in the conversion experience reaches beyond its immediacy through the re-ordering of values and the discernment of meaning. The desire for understanding augments a conversion of consciousness by extending its grasp into new regions of experience. In fact, the interpretive power of the word-event must be carried by thought and action into the world of experience or else its significance will be obscured by the particularity of a single occurrence. The single occurrence announces possibilities that must be woven into the fabric of everyday life if it is to be more than an aberration of normalcy and a mere psychic curiosity. This is the theological exigency that accompanies a vital worldly ministry. Interpretation is an expression of love and care for a world of experience that has become deficient in meaning.

The familiar distinction between a prophetic and priestly ministry is elaborated by the concept of ministry as a practical hermeneutic. Interpretation under the aegis of a new principle of reality is implicitly if not explicitly a critique of culture and its institutions. Old perceptions must be adjusted to the eschatological reality of the word-event. What may have been limiting experiences on the horizon of experience are now moved toward the foreground of experience when viewed under an ultimate horizon. Conversion sanctions radical questioning of the depth and density of ideological and cultural institutions because they cannot appear as ultimate. A prophetic ministry is concerned with "telling the truth" by establishing the place of real experiences in relationship to our vision of ultimate reality. The critique of culture is the preliminary formulation of a new ethic. The granting of a place for the particularities of experience through interpretation reveals incongruities and injustices that call us into action. Dietrich Bonhoeffer, in his *Ethics*, has suggested that "telling the truth" is "saying how something is in reality."[17] This includes respect for concealment and silence when it serves this purpose. We may wish to add that "doing the truth" is a consent to reality through the interpretive processes of thought and action.

The critical function of a prophetic ministry is actually the foundation for a priestly ministry. "Telling the truth" undermines false structures that inhibit and wound the search for wholeness. The healing function of priestly ministry is manifested through the introduction of depth and the discernment of ultimate meaning in the interpretive probing of everyday experience. Interpretation even generates a language through which important relationships can be tentatively explored and brought to realization. The imagination increasingly can seek wholeness unfettered by the limitations of shallow talk and impotent language. Thus, interpretation is a practical necessity for any ministry that seeks to intensify joy and discern meaning in suffering by lifting the individuality of experience into a story of ultimate significance. Many people have a difficult time living their normal lives. The critical function of interpretation prepares a priestly ministry to accept people and understand them on a deeper level than they understand themselves. Priestly ministry should seek visible expression for a deeper interpretation of existence that challenges complacency with surface understanding and also orients consciousness toward the possibility for new understanding. Ritual and sacrament particularize the symbolic power of language in the word-event. Interpretation transforms the world into a sacrament so that sacred and secular meanings are symbolically fused in the unity of experience.

---

[17]Dietrich Bonhoeffer, *Ethics* (New York: Macmillan Paperback Edition, 1965), p. 372.

Practical hermeneutics implies a new agenda for the ministry. There will always be a new agenda for the ministry because the word of God directs us out of the sanctuary into the world it interprets. There is no simple formula for answering the call to ministry. Ministry is an open-ended vocation. Its implementation will be relative to the world that it serves, but its source and its power will be the vision of a new reality that is of ultimate significance.

This chapter has appeared previously as an article in the ANGLICAN THEOLOGICAL REVIEW, and appears here with the permission of the *ATR* editors.

Chapter Two

SYMBOL AND STORY

We have clearly arrived at the understanding that the new agenda for ministry arises out of the transformation of consciousness. The practical problem for the implementation of this agenda is that a large portion of it is hidden in the tacit dimensions of a new consciousness. Practical hermeneutics and theoretical hermeneutics complement each other in exploring the wholeness of experience and the foundational contrasts that make a new consciousness possible and enrich the relationships of consciousness to the world.

The intuition of depth that accompanies a conversion is a positive affirmation, but it is also a problem for delineating the new agenda for ministry. There is an involvement with a deeper layer of meaning that is not explicit. It is actually a reflection of the nature of consciousness itself and not the peculiar property of a conversion experience. In a simplified description of the structure of consciousness we know that consciousness requires a pattern of contrast for its existence. Consciousness involves comparative discriminations even when we are referring to the simple perception of color or form. Perceptual consciousness of particular objects is a privileged mental process that can emerge only when a contrast established between object and ground is sufficiently vivid to be effectively present. Consciousness can be viewed as a privileged event because not all mental processes cross the threshold of consciousness. The consciousness of meaning is a complex parallel process that represents an achievement. Patterns of relationship that signify meaning can be present to consciousness only as a contrast is established within a realm of other possibilities.[1] This act of consciousness is larger than its content and

[1] The foundational structures that establish the possibility for consciousness can be explored through transcendental inquiry. See Charles E. Winquist, *The Transcendental Imagination* (The Hague: Martinus Nijhoff, 1972) and *The Communion of Possibility* (Chico: New Horizons Press, 1975), Chapter IV.

is enriched by the possibilities and unconscious processes out of which it emerges. These possibilities and processes are part of what we mean by the tacit dimension of consciousness. There is a sense in which these possibilities house a hidden agenda for the future of experience. A new consciousness is intuitively related to the deeper level of resources that are at its foundation even though they do not explicitly manifest themselves. The surface expression of consciousness is a veiled announcement that there are meanings that belong to experience that have not yet been plumbed.

The possibilities for the definition of the ministerial agenda are so far-ranging that we are tempted to halt before their immensity. It is easy to become mired in the ambiguity of decision-making as we confront the complexity of massive social institutions. We need a plan that will make the task of explicating the new agenda for the ministry manageable but that is not reductive or destructive of the consciousness that we seek to understand. The new world born in the matrix of transformed consciousness presents an unlimited range of possibilities for interpretation. Its cosmic proportions and organic complexity challenge the adequacy of any method of interpretation. We must learn how to focus on our task through the limitations of a human eye. Plato is confronted with a similar problem in *The Republic* when Socrates seeks a visible image of justice in his dialogue with Glaucon and Adeimantos.[2] He suggests that, if we are trying to read an inscription written in small letters at a distance, we would be fortunate to be able to find the same inscription in larger letters somewhere else. We could then read the inscription in larger letters and compare it with the inscription in smaller letters. Socrates then seeks to understand the justice of the individual person as it is comparatively illuminated by the justice of a city. Our problem is not that the letters of a hidden ministerial agenda are written too small, but that they are so large that we are not able to bring them into purview of our finite vision. Perhaps we can be aided by looking at the presentation of possibilities as they are written small. The microcosm belongs to the macrocosm; and, no matter where we begin, the privilege of consciousness will be implicated in the whole. Plato looked at the city to find a clue to the concept of justice in the individual. We will look at the individual to see if we can discover a clue to the concept of the ministry in the "city." The proportions in a search for understanding the individual are more immediately manageable but are no less complex than the whole of reality of which they are an expression.

---

[2]Plato, *The Great Dialogues of Plato* (New York: Mentor Books, 1956), p. 165.

John Dunne quotes from *Moby Dick* an exclamation of Ahab that reveals an even more important reason for beginning with an investigation of the human story as a paradigm for the definition of ministry. Ahab says, "Let me look into a human eye. . . . It is better than to gaze into the sea or sky, better than to gaze upon God."[3] Dunne suggests that by looking into a human eye the wild and dark powers that are at work in the cosmos are seen as integral to our humanity. The privilege of consciousness should be allied with the power of consent to our humanity. When the mystery of the unknown is framed in human dimensions, we can assess the meaning of a decision for the integration of new possibilities into the human agenda. The ghosts of new possibilities are not obscure judgments on the adequacy of experience but are representations of an invitation into a fuller complex of experiences when they are integrated into the search for self-understanding.

Practical hermeneutics can begin by looking at individual stories. The alliance of practical hermeneutics with self-understanding reveals a general paradigm for the implementation of ministry. It has the advantage over global conceptions of ministry by establishing its significance in the realm of immediate experience.

The Need for an Elementary Language of Individuation

Carl Jung relates a fascinating case study from his early work as a psychiatrist that reveals a fundamental issue that often blocks processes of self-realization. We cannot explore the meaning of the self unless we have a language that is adequate for this task. In this particular case study, Jung was working with a very intelligent and enlightened Jewish woman. The woman had been suffering from a severe anxiety neurosis for years. Jung's analysis was preceded by an interesting dream that suggested to him that she might have an unusual father complex. In actual analysis he was not able to detect a father complex and began to inquire about her grandfather. Her resistance betrayed the confidentiality of her feelings, and Jung pursued the story of her grandfather until he had established that the grandfather was a zaddick in the Hasidim. The woman was astounded when Jung told her that the root of her neurosis was the fear of God. The neurosis disappeared in a week according to the account given by Jung. He concluded that he had to awaken religious and mythological ideas in her because "she had no mythological ideas, and therefore the most essential feature of her

---

[3]John S. Dunne, *Time and Myth* (Notre Dame: University of Notre Dame Press Edition, 1975), p. 47.

nature could find no way to express itself."[4] This case study is enlarged by the philosophical insight that descriptive and ostensive language functions are complemented by a heuristic function that anticipates the intelligibility of what is to be experienced and known. If our language is shallow and impotent, we feel that we are chained to describing the surface of experience. We feel that we have lost our freedom.

In a situation with highly visible constraints, the concept of freedom that develops is usually defined in terms of the removal of external constraints. This is only a partial concept. The actualization of freedom is also an affirmation of possibilities. These possibilities must be presented to consciousness so that with the increment of the future they can in fact be realized. This does not mean that freedom is not first a removal of oppressive constraints. The removal of external constraints is often necessary before we can enlarge the concept of freedom. That is, external constraints can be the first problem for the enjoyment of freedom. However, the meaning of freedom is submerged unless we are then able to make a choice among possibilities that stand before consciousness. This of course means that before freedom can be positively valued and enjoyed, new possibilities must be imaginatively entertained in consciousness. In our society there are large numbers of people that live without excessive external constraints in the determination of their lives. However, the failure of the imagination to present a wide range of possibilities to consciousness is experienced as a loss of freedom. The cumulative effect of imaginative failure is a pervasive sense of boredom and a resultant dependency upon public entertainment to sustain interest in life. The conscious valuation of freedom is sometimes lost in this transition. Capitulation to hours of television viewing and the familiar Sunday afternoon dilemma—What shall we do?—are simple expressions of what it means to lose touch with the imaginative foundations of freedom. Liberation from manipulative and coercive forces is only the first step on the road to freedom. The language of freedom must be a language of possibility. Freedom from inhibiting constraints is important but it is not identical with the achievement of freedom in the realization of individual identity.

Without the imaginative entertainment of possibilities in consciousness the concept of freedom appears artificial or is internalized and felt as a harsh judgment against the achievement of selfhood. The dilemma of freedom illuminates the need for a language that announces the presence of real possibilities before

---

[4]Carl G. Jung, *Memories, Dreams, Reflections* (New York: Vintage Book, 1963), pp. 138–39.

the eye of consciousness in processes of individuation. When Jung realized that it was necessary to awaken religious and mythological ideas in his patient, he understood that a language of possibility was necessary for her to be free from her neurosis and to be free to affirm the fullness of the self. On a much less profound level, we can see that we must first envision the possibility for intentional action before we can even make a simple decision to go to the grocery store. However, we should be careful not to generalize from overly simple examples. The language of possibility must be appropriate to the complexity of the emergent occasion of experience. Language nourishes the growth of experience on all levels of conscious achievement.

Any expulsion of religious discourse from the marketplace of sober thinking is naturally accompanied by a diminution of religious experience and a loss of freedom. The desire for meaningful understanding and experience that reaches beyond the ordinary use of language would be frustrated by the resultant impoverishment of the imagination. When examining individual experience the loss of religious language rich in possibilities is a loss of freedom that frustrates individuation processes. It can even assume the proportions of an anxiety neurosis as exemplified in the case study of the Jewish woman related by Jung. In the analysis of individual experience we can clearly assess the importance of religio-mythological language and there discover our first important clue for a practical revision of the concept of the ministry. One of the functions of ministry is to make religious language available to the dynamic life of the community. This task is not simple. It is not identical with the construction of a theological dictionary. Language can extend the privilege of consciousness only if it can be integrated into the flow of present experience. Few contemporary men and women are informed by the mighty acts of God as expressed in their biblical and mythological dress. Traditional religio-mythological language must be revalorized if it is to contribute to processes of individuation at the heart of human experience. The first language that promotes self-consciousness is autobiographical and confessional. The conjunction of self-transcendence with self-consciousness requires a language that is more than a rehearsal of the past. The past must be lifted up into a context that provides a more extensive pattern for reference in the determination of meaning.

The legitimacy of the autobiographical form for religious understanding is historically enfranchised by the fact of Augustine's *Confessions*. Talk of God is deeply intertwined with talk of the self. Revelation is a problem for the self. That is, the vision of a new reality requires adjustment in self-understanding. The autobiographical form points to that knowledge which appropriates talk of transcendence into self-understanding. Augustine realized that, before we can possess what we have seen and transform insight into understanding, initial insight must be embodied in our living.[5] An autobiographical story is a secondary reflection on the achievement of understanding in religious life. The inability to tell a story that is autobiographically significant can be a symptomatic expression of underdeveloped religious experience.

For many people the language of confession is not easily transformed into the narrative expression of a story. It is often difficult to see patterns emerge from what is sometimes experienced as disconnected events. The advantage of starting with the immediacy of autobiographical experience is that it is both important and real to us. However, everyday experiences are often accented by a familiar sense of reality without being understood as important. When this happens, the sense of importance is then attached to the need to make these experiences intelligible in a framework of larger significance. There is a desire to work through experience so that it is lifted into a context of greater significance that in turn becomes an extension of the experience. The process of interpretation can be an appropriation of meaning. Interpretation gives a voice to experience so that its significance can be heard and made a part of our conscious identity. This means that the voice of experience must speak on a frequency that is within the receptive thresholds of the listener.

Beginning with a personal confession anchors interpretation in conscious experience. This experience can be used as a further reference for the elaboration of meanings. The witness of a community of faith to an individual can have a psychological urgency if it is interpretively related to even a fragmented awareness of the personal story of the individual. Ministry must acknowledge the individuality of experience in the adjudication of reality if it is to be effective. Ministry can become skewed and defensive if it loses sight of the psychological urgency of its voice.

There are two intriguing definitions of God from the history of theology that illustrate the psychological need for religious language and provide a clue to the concept of ministry as a practical hermeneutic. The first is from Anselm's *Proslogion*. Anselm explores the interiority of experience with such force that he cannot be ignored even if we are comfortable with a childhood conception of God. It would be possible to reject Anselm's ontological arguments for the existence of God and still feel the

[5]David B. Burrell, *Exercises in Religious Understanding* (Notre Dame: University of Notre Dame Press, 1974), p. 22.

psychological significance of his conception of God. To acknowledge that we can formulate our understanding of God as "that than which nothing greater can be conceived" challenges the adequacy of any other formulation of the concept of God that is narrower and less inclusive. If our God does not measure up to this formula, then it is difficult to understand why our concept of God is an acceptable focal point for worship. That is, it is difficult to understand how anyone could orient their lives around a concept that is not "that than which nothing greater can be conceived." To acknowledge that there is a notion of God that surpasses the object of our worship is to supplant the present object of worship with the greater concept.

Anselm begins his quest for understanding within the circle of faith, but his formulation of transcendence even challenges the adequacy of secular consciousness. If we begin our inquiry without a concept of God, Anselm's formulation forces us toward a conception of God unless we are so positivistic in our attitudes that we dismiss our own abilities to conceptualize as nonsensical. Anselm's formulation of his understanding of God is a question directed to modern experience even if it fails to be an answer. To argue that the formula is an empty structure without content is actually a confession that modern experience has stopped short of its own ability to become conscious of what it conceives to be of greatest significance. Once Anselm implicitly formulates the question, we are under an obligation to answer it or else we must admit that we are unwilling to ask the question. The choice not to think about "that than which nothing greater can be conceived" has psychological and philosophical implications. Anselm's concept of God is an abstract expression of the unrestricted desire for understanding. To deny the question that is implicit in his simple formulation of the concept of God is a choice against the conscious experience of an unrestricted desire for understanding. The loss is experiential. It is not surprising that if we decide to restrict inquiry, then understanding will be impoverished and experience will be reduced to commonplace occurrences. Psychological need to explore "that than which nothing greater can be conceived" preempts philosophical justifications to limit inquiry to what is clear and distinct. Self-understanding begins in the middle of experience, and Anselm's concept of God is a simple amplification of our ability to raise a question in the middle of our experience.[6]

In modern theological dress we discover a parallel to Anselm's formula in Paul Tillich's concept of God as the object of our ultimate concern. Tillich's assertion that "faith is the state of being ultimately

---

[6]*Ibid.*, cf. Chapter 2, pp. 45–79.

concerned: the dynamics of faith are the dynamics of man's ultimate concern" is an affirmation that people are capable of taking something seriously without reservation.[7] The object of our ultimate concern can be no less than "that than which nothing greater can be conceived." Tillich notes that, if the object of our ultimate concern is less than "that than which nothing greater can be conceived," then the quality of our living is dimmed and shrouded by disappointment.[8]

Tillich's sermon "The Depth of Existence" is a powerful expression of the psychological exigency in religious thought.[9] He is aware that the surface of experience is not satisfying and that we seek a depth of meaning that can satisfy our desires for a knowledge of the self that is important and substantial. What we mean by the word *God* can be no less than the concern for depth in our lives. He says that "if you know that God means depth . . . you cannot call yourself an atheist or unbeliever. For you cannot think or say: Life has no depth! Life itself is shallow."[10] His claim that you cannot think that life has no depth and is shallow is a psychological and existential claim. If we can comfortably say that life has no depth, then Tillich's thought loses its psychological urgency and Anselm's concept of God is trivialized. There are, however, very few people who are willing to say that life has no depth. A more common confession is that "I have not been able to discover depth and significance in my life." If this is our confession, then Anselm's concept of God and Tillich's definition of faith as ultimate concern are challenges to the complacency of living only on the surface of life.

The importance of Anselm's and Tillich's formulations is that they demonstrate a need even in the heart of secular experience to talk about God if we are to take account of the realities and possibilities for self-affirmation. The immediate reference for religious inquiry is the affirmation of our own power to think and raise limiting questions that point beyond the boundaries of conventional experience. The dilemma that surrounds the acknowledgment that Anselm and Tillich have focused on the psychological need to conceive of God at the center of human experience is that we have no language readily available to us to serve this need. The collapse of naive belief in the face of modern historical and scientific studies was accompanied by the loss of the

---

[7]Paul Tillich, *Dynamics of Faith* (New York: Harper Torchbook Edition, 1958), p. 1.
[8]*Ibid.*, p. 12.
[9]Paul Tillich, *The Shaking of the Foundations* (New York: Charles Scribner's Sons, 1948), pp. 52–63.
[10]*Ibid.*, p. 57.

language that expressed that belief. When religious language loses its symbolic power it is trivialized and relegated to the periphery of life in museums and sanctuaries.

"That than which nothing greater can be conceived" becomes a psychological aporia without religio-mythological symbols as vessels to house the imagination. We are at an impasse. We experience a need that we do not know how to meet. The imagination needs a medium to transform the possible into the actual. Language is not the only medium available to the imagination, but it is closely associated with the privilege of consciousness. The symbolic function is not always conscious. Mircea Eliade reminds us that it is the lesson of depth psychology that a symbol can deliver its message even when its meaning escapes the conscious mind.[11] Consciousness can be satisfied in its talk of God only if a sufficient contrast can be established to engender conscious appreciation of the symbolic function. The genius of language is that the propositional structure can be a conjunctive form that entertains contrasts in a unified expression. However, the formal possibility for religious consciousness does not guarantee its realization. The experiential unity of "I think" and "I am" can be a circle reinforcing the affirmations of a believer, but it can also be a circle excluding the participation of the nonbeliever in traditional religio-mythological symbols. The return to precritical belief is impossible for a modern man or woman because it alienates them from the immediacy of the empirical self that is an essential element in any meaningful affirmation of the unity between "I think" and "I am." Individuation and integration are indivisible processes and cannot progress from the separation of thinking from its empirical reference points. We cannot get behind, below, above, or beyond conscious experience without going through consciousness. Our inquiry always begins in the middle. Tillich and Anselm challenge secular consciousness precisely because they speak to the middle of experience. The only way that we can legitimately respond to the psychological urgency of their challenge is to take a hard look at the middle of experience. Perhaps that hard look will itself expand the linguistic platform on which we stand and thereby enlarge the reference for meaning.

Ambiguity, Pathology, and the Imagination

When self-understanding is intertwined with religious understanding, the common usage of language is often extended beyond

---

[11]Mircea Eliade, *The Two and the One* (New York: Harper Torchbook Edition, 1969), p. 211.

the boundaries of intelligibility. The crossing over the boundary of meaningfulness is not always noticed until the gradual diminution of meaning assumes massive proportions. One of the problems of the language of worship is that it looks so much like the ordinary use of language that we do not see the need to investigate how we can use our language in an extraordinary way without a loss of meaning. For example, if I tell you that I talked with my wife last night, this statement would not appear to be extraordinary even if you did not know me and know that I have a wife. The statement would not appear extraordinary because you know that it could be empirically verified or falsified. If, however, I claimed to have spoken with George Washington last night, you might suspect that I was using language differently. Confessional statements about talking with God resemble my second example more than the first even though all three examples are grammatically similar. A broad familiarity with vocabulary and grammar does not guarantee clarity and meaning. If we are unwilling to dismiss statements that do not meet the verifiability criterion for meaning as meaningless, then we must expand the meaning of meaning itself. That is, we must discern multiple functions for language usage. If we rush to the boundaries of language to make this determination, we are in danger of confusing the *content* of extraordinary uses of language with the *use* of the language because it is unfamiliar territory. It is better if we begin our inquiry in the middle of experience.

Even in the ordinary use of language the rules for usage are not always clear, and language can become problematic. Philosophical attempts to create a calculus of language that eliminates ambiguity have always been frustrated. In fact, some of the most profound insights into the multiplicity of language-games have come from philosophers who sought a language of univocal expression. For example, Ludwig Wittgenstein has stated very clearly "that the *speaking* of language is part of an activity, or of a form of life."[12] Language has as many voices as it has uses in the diverse activities of life. The desire for simplicity and clarity is shipwrecked on the complexities of ordinary experience even without an appeal to mysteries at the boundaries of experience.

This epistemological dilemma can be the foundation of a psychological hope if we feel trapped in a language-game that speaks only of the surfaces of experience. The suggestion that language has multiple functions confuses consciousness but also extends its range into new patterns of relationship or meaning. If consciousness can take account of the presence of multiple

---

[12]Ludwig Wittgenstein, *Philosophical Investigations* (Oxford: Basil Blackwell, 1967), p. 11.

meanings in a unitary expression, there is an intersection of levels of meaning that cannot be explained with reference only to the surface of experience. The ambiguities and ambivalences in language need not be an occasion of philosophical frustration. They are an announcement of possibilities and lay open the task of interpretation.

The discovery of the symbol is a crack in the surface of experience. This crack is threatening when we are satisfied with the depth that we have achieved in our understanding. The symbol can be simply defined as an expression that has more than one meaning. The discovery of the symbol is the recognition that some expressions are inherently ambiguous because they are valenced for more than one pattern of meaning. We can say that they are ambivalent or even multivalent. This does not mean that we lack rigor or logical acumen in our thinking. It means that some expressions or images touch a variety of levels of experience and can function simultaneously on multiple levels. We do not have to go to the edges of language to discover symbols. The simple perception of a color is related to both cognitive and affective experience. We cannot exhaust the meaning of "red. . ." by determining its place only in cognitive discourse or only in affective experience. We implicitly acknowledge the symbolic function in language every time we are disappointed by interpretation on a single level and think that it is not satisfactory because there is more going on in a particular experience than can be accounted for on a single level of interpretation.

The careful listening to the voices of language leads to recognition that symbols are overdetermined. That is, they are related to more than one realm of discourse and meaning. They have multiple functions in the scheme of experience. This means that any interpretation must be an overinterpretation. We must allow the symbol to lead thinking onto different levels of significance. This admittedly obscures surface interpretations, but the loss of clarity is a gain in depth. This statement should not be misconstrued as an obscurantist's manifesto. The commitment of empiricism to experience is not a commitment to simplicity. The interpretive measure of experience must be adequate to the complexity of experience. Ambiguity and ambivalence are not always faults in language that must be eliminated. Except in those cases where ambiguity is a result of sloppy thinking, the presence of ambiguity and ambivalence announces the symbolic function even in the middle of ordinary language usage. A door is opened that we can pass through on the way to self-understanding.

The symbol is a coincidence of meanings that generates a gain in consciousness by naturally entertaining contrasts in its simplest expression. For example, from the common associations of water as cleanliness or nourishment and as deluge or chaos to the mystical coincidence of opposites, the symbol is a bearer of new consciousness and new experience. It is a passageway and a point of conjunction that links the primitive speech of desire with high ethical ideals. The symbol reveals that every individual is living a multiplicity of stories that consciously intersect in the function of the symbol. Without the overinterpretation of symbolic language the presence of the symbol frustrates understanding.

Overinterpretation is the implementation of a practical hermeneutic. It is basically attending to the many voices of the symbol in everyday life. The work of overinterpretation does not dispense with the symbolic function, but it is a conscious acknowledgment and accounting for the presence of the symbol.

There is no formula for overinterpretation. If a symbol is valenced on many levels, it will be necessary to enter into diverse forms of discourse for the determination of meaning. The range of overinterpretation can be inclusive of polar opposites. The symbol may direct us toward meanings that lie below it in the unconscious. The deepest level of interpretation for a particular experience may speak of both ethereal and atavistic identifications. In every instance, the symbolic function is not identical with its multiple interpretations. The meaning of the symbol is always part of the conjunctive act that is its power and use in language.

The symbol remains a shadow in the development of a theory of interpretation. Overinterpretation cannot eliminate the symbol because the symbol has a unique function. As a conjunctive point where diverse uses of language intersect, its significance cannot be fully determined in any one interpretive framework. Multiple interpretations help us understand the importance of the symbolic function, but the symbol is valenced differently for each of the patterns. The overlay of patterns on each other would be a falsification of experience. The genius of the symbol is that it makes a conjunction that does not dissolve the tension and difference between the polarities of experience. Creation is not identical with destruction but in the symbolic function these polarities can be held in tension. In the symbolic function we are also able to preserve the differences among cosmological, theological, psychological, and biological meanings and still acknowledge that a single symbol can work on all of these levels. The symbol can facilitate movement from one level of interpretation to another without distorting the integrity of interpretation on any of its functioning levels. That is, I do not have to reduce or transform theology into psychology to explain how a theological concept is intimately a part of my psychological experience. It is clear that a symbolic idea functions on both levels and can be interpreted on both levels. The integration occurs in the symbol itself and not in forcing one pattern of interpretation on another. The discovery that an individual is living a multiplicity of stories on different levels does not dissolve the significance of any one of those stories. I do not mean to suggest that the symbolic conjunction is not important and influential in all of the affected patterns of interpretation. For example, both theology and psychology must be responsive to the symbolic coincidence of the search for God and the search for self or they individually become deficient in meaning. If the symbol becomes anomalous for any delineation of meaning, consciousness falters and experience is obscured on that level of interpretation. When we allow for the symbol to announce its multiple voices, interpretation on one level provides access to other levels of interpretation that might not have been readily available. In the development of a practical hermeneutic we quickly realize that to tell a story on one level can help us discover and enter into a story on another level.

This insight can lead us in a variety of directions. It is possible that telling the story of ourselves in a psychological idiom will provide access to the significance of mythological and theological stories, or we may be moving in the other direction and discover access to our highly personal story by telling mythological stories of the mighty acts of God or gods. For example, the resonances between the drama of Oedipus and the story of ourselves that have long been acknowledged in psychoanalytic thought can be double vectored. We can move through this opening in either direction. We may have a better appreciation of our personal story as it is illuminated by the story of Oedipus; or, by understanding the depth of our personal story, we can gain access to the far-reaching implications of mythological struggles in Greek tragedy. Psychological adventures into the realm of myth through the symbolic function are enlargements of consciousness and spaces for the imagination to express itself.

We can affirm that ambiguity and ambivalence can be a road to imaginative freedom that begins in the middle of ordinary experience. However, this beginning in the middle is not always a straightforward revelation of new possibilities. One of the unique characteristics of the symbol is that it can be used to mask as well as to reveal. Symbolism can be abstruse so that, even though it signifies or reveals a point of conjunction with other patterns of meaning, it remains obscure on the first level of experience and actually frustrates the development of conscious understanding. This "pathology" is not without significance. The anomaly of the symbol can enlarge and pervade the total sense of conscious experience. Distortion and disguise have an etiology that can be untangled if we work through the experience with courage and care. The symbol cannot mask without also revealing that there are areas of experience that have not been integrated into self-understanding. Illness, deformity, disguise, and abnormality are all meaningful attendants to the surface of experience and can become voices from the depths of the soul. They provide space on the surface of experience for the expression of other, sometimes unconscious, patterns of meaning. It is James Hillman's suggestion that we regard "pathologizing" as a mode of speech that uses a magnified and misshapen language.[13]

The story that is told through pathology is difficult to interpret, but it cannot be ignored without a loss of depth in our understanding of personal development. Pathology shatters the pretensions of completeness and adequacy of interpretation on a single level of experience. Deeper levels of meaning force themselves symptomatically into consciousness.[14] Pathologies can be alienated stories that establish a grotesque contrast with the normality of consciousness. If new consciousness is engendered, the pathologized experience is an imaginative achievement shadowed by the suffering that accompanies its realization.

It is important to note that neurosis is not usually valued as an imaginative achievement. It would be naive to underestimate the destructive qualities of neurotic behavior. When pathology provides the vessel for an expression of depth, there is an implied suggestion that no other vessel is available.

The interpretation of language-usage as an event provides a clue to understanding why pathology is necessary to announce hidden meanings. The flattening of language has been assumed to be a symptom of neurosis. This view fails to understand the dynamic quality of the language-event in the generation of consciousness. The conjunctive structure of language or its analogies lie at the foundation of consciousness by providing the possibility for contrast. When language is denied its multiple functions, effective contrast is eliminated from feeling and consciousness dims. The anomaly of the symbol fractures the unity of surface consciousness, and stable behavior patterns are threatened by disorder. The withdrawal from consciousness is considered to be neurotic. The emergence of visible pathological images challenges the withdrawal from consciousness through distortion and disproportion. The illness becomes the language available to consciousness. If we are clever, our pathologies can be masked as mysteries of the soul.

---

[13]James Hillman, *Re-Visioning Psychology* (New York: Harper & Row, 1975), p. 82.
[14]Cf. *ibid.*, p. 104.

However, there is at the base of the pathology a failure of language to house the contrast necessary for imaginative consciousness. The pathological expression is an inadequate alternative for a rich symbolic language. Consciousness becomes self-alienated as it is imbedded and lost in a pathological container. Pathology can absorb the imagination so that consciousness loses its natural reflexivity. The self no longer possesses its own meaning. This loss of meaning is a religious, not a medical, problem.

The alienation of consciousness from its own significance is not a denial of meaning. It is a loss of meaning. The specter of meaninglessness casts many shadows over the analysis of experience. On a primary level there are relationships that surround the realization of consciousness of which we remain unaware. Our world extends from the immediacy of our bodies to the comprehensiveness of the cosmos. Our individual stories are bonded to the stories of our community, nation, and culture. We do not always experience the extension of ourselves to cosmological proportions because we have no language that can entertain these possibilities and still be identified with our immediate empirical consciousness. In the midst of this pervasive unconscious state we can only postulate that there are dimensions to our lives that remain unknown. In this instance the concept of the unconscious refers to the vast unknown world that surrounds us. Because of our conscious achievements we become vaguely aware that consciousness has faltered before the fullness of reality and is fallible.

The alienation of consciousness is different from the simple state of being unconscious. Consciousness is a privilege and depends on the establishment of contrast. Language serves consciousness as a structure that can entertain contrast. There are other media that function analogously to language. However, in every instance, consciousness takes an object. That is, consciousness is intentional but it is never purely objective. The reflexive "I think" and its many perceptual variants are an existential appendage to the intentional object of consciousness. In this sense consciousness is the imaginative extension of the self. It is possible, and sometimes appears desirable, for consciousness to become totally absorbed in its object and to disguise its own character and significance as an extension of the self. We sometimes simply lose ourselves in the complexity of object relationships. The privilege of consciousness ignores the self because the object relationships exhibit an intense and vivid contrast. The "I" of the self becomes a spectator. There are other times when the extension of the self through the increase of consciousness threatens the stability and order of its past achievements. When this happens, consciousness retreats through the levels of the symbolic function to a safer depth and masks its achievement by stumbling over the ambivalence of the symbol. Consciousness is now falsified, and the imagination must seek a vessel for its expression that does not immediately refer back to the self. The vessel can be as obscure as an alchemist's crucible, as common as a dream, as painful as neurosis, or as acceptable as disciplined scholarship. In each instance, when this happens, a story is told about the self that is not e;perienced as belonging to the self.

The implementation of a practical concern for the realization of the individual is at least a twofold task. First, we need a language that is sufficiently complex to house contrast for the imaginative advance of consciousness into worlds of meaning that are a natural extension of the self. Secondly, we need to recover lost meanings that have been eliminated from conscious enjoyment by their abstraction and projection into seemingly objective interpretive patterns. The first of these tasks is a journey into philosophy, theology, and mythology. The second task is a confrontation with the shadow of our own inferiority.[15]

Spiritual Transformation

The importance that has been assigned to the symbolic function of language complicates our common understanding of what we mean by the self. Even the concept of self is overdetermined. It must be interpreted on a variety of levels. There is no single mask that can be removed to discover the true self. The most familiar paradigm for multilayered interpretation is the structural hypothesis in psychoanalytic thought defining the id, ego, and superego. The id is the psychic representative of the somatic substratum comprising instinctual forces or drives. The ego is a further differentiation detailing the relationship of id forces to environmental objects as manifested in consciousness. The superego is a differentiation within the ego function that accounts for the internalization of parental and cultural values. The self cannot be identified with any one of these distinct functions. The self is an encompassing concept that is differentiated by function in the structural hypothesis. The structural hypothesis is a preliminary accounting for the complexity of empirical experience. Because these are provisional definitions they are not philosophically finalized even though it may be very useful in a clinical situation to assume their closure. Functional definitions are always secondary to

---

[15]In Jungian psychology the first of these tasks would be a journey into the collective psyche and the second a confrontation with the personal unconscious that is symbolically expressed in relationship to the archetype of the shadow.

experience and are open to revision and elaboration if they do not account for experience. This means that the role of functional definition is primarily methodological. It renders observation more acute by mapping out an area of inquiry as well as providing a language for interpretation in that area of experience. If we choose to extend inquiry, we must also further refine and expand our language. The structural hypothesis focuses on consciousness, secondary process thinking, and its interrelationship with the semantics of desire, primary process thinking. The distinction between primary process and secondary process thinking can be further augmented by a tertiary component that refers to the consciousness of conscious experience.

Practical hermeneutics aims at a recovery of the whole self. We are in search of a soul and a spirit. The revision of psychology is complemented by a revision of theology. The pneumatic augments the psychic if we adopt the concept of spirit to the structural hypothesis as a fourth functional differentiation of the self. We cannot ignore the bodily substratum of experience, but we also cannot ignore the increment in experience that occurs when consciousness reflects on itself. The concept of spirit can be functionally defined so that it refers to a differentiation of experience and not to a ghost in the machine. If we acknowledge that consciousness is a privileged occasion and that ego-consciousness is a functional notation for the relationship of primary instinctual forces to the environment, it is merely an extension of our definitional capability to speak of the spirit as the secondary relationship that consciousness establishes with immediate conscious experience. This definition of spirit is simply a further differentiation of the privilege of consciousness so that our basic understanding can descriptively incorporate the complexity of conscious experience. Consciousness of an object is the first meaning of empirical experience, but consciousness of consciousness is a relationship to experience that is also an experience in itself. This reflective consciousness assigns meaning to meaning. The self transcends its immediacy through this further differentiation of function.

Spirit is not a neutral term. It has been used in religious and mythological traditions and is itself a symbol. The functional definition of spirit is an exploratory concept within the scope of secular understanding. It is a provisional delimitation to provide entry into a circle of disclosure contained in the power of the symbol.

John Dunne has suggested a parallel definition by referring to spirit as an overtone of experience. "Every human thing—childhood, youth, manhood, and age, life, action, and love—is like a complex musical tone comprising a fundamental tone, the thing itself, and an overtone, one's relationship to the thing."[16] Spirit is the overtone in the quest for life. It can be created or remain as an unrealized possibility. Thus, the formation of spirit can be retarded and distorted by the restriction of reflective consciousness. Consciousness can create a world of meaning by standing in relationship to its own immediacy. The first meaning of spirit is the unique achievement of reflective consciousness. However, the material of primary consciousness is transformed into spirit without losing its own meaning. The self gains a spirit that transcends its origin. An elementary analogy is established between what Nikos Kazantzakis has called our highest obligation: "the obligation to transubstantiate the matter which God entrusted to us, and turn it into spirit"[17] and what Carl Jung has called the sole purpose of human existence: the creation of "more and more consciousness."[18]

Interpretation is substantially more than an academic exercise. It is the overtone of our reading a text or standing in the middle of experience. Interpretation is a spiritual exercise. Spirit is the substance of reflective consciousness. Interpretation is the work of reflective consciousness. Spirit is endangered if the work of reflective consciousness is frustrated.

We can now expand our understanding of Jung's case study of the young woman who had no mythological ideas. Without a mythic-symbolic language consciousness was restricted to a one-dimensional interpretation of experience. The most essential feature of her nature, her spirit, had no substance and density. Personality development faltered in the artificial restriction of consciousness. She had no language available to her that could entertain the contrasts necessary for expansion of consciousness and the creation of spirit. Traditional analysis would not have opened the door to self-understanding. Jung opened the door to a future achievement by consciousness, by introducing her to the world of spirit. The isolation of the woman from mythic-symbolic language rich in possibility was a causal factor in her anxiety neurosis. Consciousness could not escape its immediacy because no other level of meaning reflected its achievement. Her individual story needed to be integrated into a larger context to advance the achievement of consciousness. Without mythological ideas and symbolic language she had no vessel that could house a larger story. Her intellectual life was one-dimensional and did not provide

[16]Dunne, p. 21.
[17]Nikos Kazantzakis, Saint Francis (New York: Ballantine Books, 1966), p. 7.
[18]Jung, p. 326.

access to the imagination. Her anxiety neurosis was the symptom and not the cause of her inability to grasp what was real and important in her life.

It is very easy to confuse the failure of consciousness to advance through a creative vision of possibilities with neurosis. The symptoms are not always distinguishable and sometimes, as is suggested in the example above, the neurosis is itself a symptom of consciousness faltering in the shallowness of its linguistic tools. A young theologian related a dream to me that further illustrates the difficulty in untangling the inhibitions of personal, feeling-toned complexes from the need for insight and understanding of the symbolic function in consciousness.

This man had been raised in a home that cherished conservative religious values and espoused a fundamentalist theology. His mother was a very strong force in his childhood; and, as he came into adulthood, he conceived of himself as suffering from a mother complex. He was familiar with psychological literature and sought to understand the psychodynamics of his own history. He recognized projections and his own inability to test reality but was unable to resolve the conflict with the projected mother image or with his actual mother.

When he began to feel that he was losing his freedom and endangering important personal relationships, he had a dream that provided a new orientation to the problem. The dream began with his standing before a large cathedral that was partially buried in the earth. His father was a watchman at the entrance of the cathedral, and the theologian passed into a labyrinth of halls and adjoining rooms. He then exited onto an alley and crossed into an older building. He entered a room of old acquaintances from his religious childhood that he had long since abandoned. He seated himself as his childhood pastor was preparing to show an evangelistic film. With an increasing sense of his own responsibility he confronted the pastor by tearing the film. The frames that he had removed from the film were a sequence of images portraying the fall of his mother. He awoke with a feeling of relief and liberation.

The dream and his associations with specific images shifted his perspective on his personal story and struggle. His father stood outside the entrance to the cathedral that sharply contrasted with the country churches of his childhood. That is, his father stood at the opening of the labyrinth of his theological education but did not enter into it. The whole process of theological education was partially buried in unconscious motivations that were psychologically adjacent to what he had experienced as a mother complex. The resolution of the mother complex required that the theologian take responsibility for the unconscious labyrinth through which he had passed. The ostensible problem was a mother complex, but the resolution was a serious appropriation of his own work. The overwhelming feeling of constraint and the loss of freedom had become symptoms of the disconnection between thought and life. The theologian had at his hand powerful tools for telling his story. The dream told him that it was time to shift from an adolescent crisis to the adult problem of meaning.

Both of the examples that we have examined reveal the need for attending to the development of the spirit as a fundamental concern of adult life. Consciousness needed to be turned around so that it looked toward expanded possibilities for the integration of experience. In both examples there was an invitation extended to explore a realm of meanings that transcended the historical immediacy of conscious experience. The immediate problems descended through the fissure in consciousness into a larger and more complex frame of reference.

Practical hermeneutics is not simply a secondary analysis of what is given. The prophetic function of ministry is integrated with the priestly function. Proclamation reveals new possibilities that alter the givenness of the conscious situation. For example, in Christian preaching the announcement that the kingdom of God is breaking into history even though it has not been earned alters our frame of reference for the interpretation of personal problems. In the example of the theologian the power of the mother was diffused in the larger context of theological reflection. The size of the problem was actually diminished relative to the larger world of meanings presented through a serious appropriation of his own theological work. The anxiety neurosis of the Jewish woman was caused by the inability to carry thinking into a larger context. In her case it was Jung who invited her into a new world of meanings that was a natural part of her cultural inheritance. In both examples consciousness was challenged by the possibility of conceiving of "that than which nothing greater can be conceived." It was the reorientation toward the promise of deeper meaning that gave permission to reach beyond the shadow of neurosis toward a larger story.

Spirit in the World

The natural events of everyday life have been revealed to be the substance of a larger story. Through myth and symbol, consciousness can come to stand in relationship with itself and be creative of the human spirit. Spirit is in the world, for it is a reflexive connection with the actual passage of experience. Where there is immediate conscious experience there is also the possibility for consciousness to determine a relationship to that experience of itself. Such a relationship is a further differentiation of self-consciousness. It is neither automatic nor necessary for mere survival. Spirit can remain buried in the objectivity of experience. Spirit is a function of the psyche that adds meaning to meaning. It is an increment of experience that fills life with new meanings. The generation of spirit approximates a fulfillment of human hope.

Ministry as a practical hermeneutic attends to the reality of the vision that transforms the matter of everyday life into spirit. There is a re-visioning of the concept of ministry when we take account of the emergence of spirit. The hermeneutical task of the ministry is threefold.

First, ministry accepts the givenness of experience. There can be no meaningful understanding of the spirit that is not rooted in the availability of ordinary experience. It is the wounding of the surface of experience that is the first clue to possibilities for the generation of the spirit. The inadequacy of a one-dimensional interpretation of experience and its inability to account for the symbolic function is revealed by closely attending to the voices that speak out of the middle of life. Ministry accepts its prophetic function when it challenges thinking by revealing its inadequacy to thematize and articulate its own significance when restricted to one level of interpretation. When the prophet cries repentance in the wilderness of life, we are called to take ourselves seriously. This prophetic voice is resisted because the illumination of understanding casts the shadow of our inferiority.

The prophetic ministry will be resisted unless it speaks compellingly about the actual shape of experience. It is only when we come to recognize that not listening to the prophetic voice will exclude us from the possibilities for self-understanding and fulfillment that we can be hearers of the word. The careful analysis of the surface of our lives is not only a judgment on the adequacy of life but also a revelation of a deeper layer of significance for life.

The second function of the ministry is to issue an invitation to share in a more satisfying vision of what is real and important in our lives. Proclamation announces that something new has entered into our experience, and we are given the choice to accept or reject what is new. Ministry must offer this possibility of turning consciousness around to re-collect our experience. Conversion and revelation coincide in the invitation to a deeper layer of interpretation. In this second function the minister is both a prophet and a priest. As a prophet, the minister proclaims that the surface of experience cannot contain the fullness of the self and that there is a greater significance to life that announces itself in the midst of our world. As a priest, the minister invites us to participate in the world of the spirit and nourishes this process by making tools available that both transcend immediate experience and reflect upon it.

The priestly task is elaborated in the third function of the ministry. The minister draws from tradition and history the symbols and mythological ideas that are necessary for the extension of consciousness in the creation of the spirit. These symbols and ideas can be interpreted and made available in communal life through teaching, preaching, sacrament, and liturgy. In the private lives of parishioners the minister can be a counselor that can risk talking about ultimate reality without the falsification of vocational commitments.

The dimly apprehended psychological need to give concrete expression to ultimate questions in the process of self-realization can be sanctioned and articulated in the life of the church if the minister accepts responsibility as an interpreter of experience and faith. Anselm's conception of God and Tillich's understanding of faith are only two examples of how a psychological need can find expression in the heritage of religious thought. Ministry serves the church and our secular culture by providing the symbols and language necessary for the imaginative advance of consciousness. As a vessel for the imagination the church is a communion of possibility.

The much maligned image of the church as a museum and guardian of tradition must be reinterpreted to be congruent with a revised concept of the ministry as practical hermeneutics. The recognition that there are multiple levels of interpretation to every life story requires that we examine the meaning of symbols and mythological ideas on a variety of levels. Although the language of religious traditions may not be usable in scientific explanation and historical description, this does not mean that it does not have a psychological and theological function. In recent theological reflections there has even been a rebirth of the gods and goddesses of polytheism and a return to the despised alchemists to discover a language that is psychologically full of meaning.[19] The gods of Mount Olympus have been dusted off, removed from the museum, and integrated into the modern imagination. James Hillman claims that "Greece persists as an inscape rather than as a landscape. . . . We return to Greece to rediscover the archetypes of our mind and our culture. . . . Greece becomes the magnifying mirror in which the psyche can recognize its persons and processes in config-

---

[19]Cf. David L. Miller, The New Polytheism: Rebirth of Gods and Goddesses (New York: Harper & Row, 1974) and Sam Keen, To a Dancing God (New York: Harper & Row, 1970).

urations which are larger than life but which bear on the life of our secondary personalities."[20] Greece has provided tools that nourish the growth of the spirit.

Greek mythology is not the only religious landscape that is a psychological inscape. The paradigmatic events and ideas that have shaped religious traditions East and West transcend the immediacy of our personal histories, magnifying and mirroring personal life. The church is more than a museum; but, as a guardian of tradition, the church is a ready retort for the alchemy of the imagination.

A ministry that attends to the great themes in religious consciousness has a language available for the telling of a story. Religion and mythology conspire against a one-dimensional interpretation of life by embodying contrasts that further consciousness. Implicit in consciousness is the question of meaning. We cannot even question the ability to question without contradiction. The question of meaning cannot be restricted without negating our own intelligence. Anselm's God is at the heart of our experience, and we have to do something about it. Consciousness is wounded by its own achievement. "That than which nothing greater can be conceived" reaches toward meanings that are psychologically larger than our immediate lives. Modern men and women are in search of a story. It is insight into the symbolic function of religio-mythological language that reveals the most profound meaning of practical hermeneutics. We tell a story in order to find a story.

---

[20]Hillman, p. 30.

Part II

PRAXIS

Chapter Three

DEPTH DIMENSIONS IN PASTORAL CARE

Practical hermeneutics is the implementation of the concern for the depth dimension in pastoral care. It is the point of conjunction for a preaching ministry that invites the community to a new vision of reality, a teaching ministry that accepts the unique history of the individual under the horizon of this new vision. The practical problem that we immediately encounter is the need for a vessel that can house this conjunctive tension in the everyday work of the ministry. Practical hermeneutics can fulfill its promise of finding a story by telling a story only if we can recognize a way to tell a story that allows for the place of the indeterminateness of possibility that surrounds the original story. Practical hermeneutics must experiment with listening to the multiple voices of symbolic thinking and find a place on the agenda of ministry to introduce the imagination into communal and individual stories.

The theoretical understanding of the integrating power of symbolic language increases our sensitivity to the need for implementing structures that make the way of symbolic thought visible, but it is not identical with these structures. Liturgical reform and the revivification of visual symbols in the work and worship of the church signify a corporate sensitivity to the need for a tangible presence of imaginative thinking. This is not enough. Ministry must bring the power of its vision into the immediate flow of everyday life. Preaching and teaching generate an expectation for meanings that could and should be woven into the fabric of individual identity. Although preaching may deliver its message, the appropriation of its meaning is a task to be worked at through teaching and counseling. At the deepest level, the growth of theological understanding, social consciousness, and collective values must coincide with a personal affirmation of meaning. This is a primary meaning of pastoral care and the particular function of pastoral counseling. However, pastoral counseling must be re-visioned to be adequate to this task.

The Recovery of Depth

The pastoral ministry must first of all recover the depth dimension of its own vocational identity. Ministry is authentic only as it attends to the profound vision of reality announced in the constellation of events that signify the meaning of conversion. Ministry is a witness to experience that is real and important. We must learn to share this witness collectively and personally. We must guard the richness of our language so that it can serve the imaginative richness of our experience. The secular paralysis of semantic anxiety is a particular danger to a ministry that is rooted in the power of the word. Where can we discover a depth in language that is responsive to the vocational calling of the ministry?

The most obvious place to look is in the traditions of the religious community, its theological reflections, and liturgical achievements. The problem with this suggestion is that the progressive secularization of culture since the Enlightenment has gradually eclipsed the primary meanings of traditional religious symbols and stories, leaving us with either a protective skepticism or a shallow literalism. In ministerial circles the loss of depth and sometimes faith has been compensated by an emerging sense of professional identity. The religious professional has a place in the secular world that is denied to the prophet. It is very seldom that the religious professional journeys into the wilderness and cries out for a more profound understanding of the human situation.

The wounded cry for a recovery of depth has not been loudly sounded in the churches and is more clearly discernible in the voices of the poor and oppressed, in asylums and consulting rooms of psychotherapists, in the fascination with the gruesome and grotesque in the public media, and even implied in exploitative images used in modern advertising. It is the secular community that has announced that it is no longer able to thematize and articulate the depth dimension in experience. The church must listen and respond to this announcement.

It is curious that in the midst of a revival of soul-searching, rumors of angels, and growing cultic communities with assorted gurus and priests, the church has too often embraced pallid images of the whole person that simply affirm that we are all okay. Part of the problem has been the isolation of theology from the parish ministry. Theology has spent so much time justifying its existence in a secular world that it has come to function under the horizon of secular thought. The renewed emphasis on hermeneutics can mark the return of an assertive theological voice. However, the concerns to which this voice will speak have now been primarily fashioned by the expressed needs of the secular world. Theology does not have to limit itself to responding to the agenda of secular thought, but it also cannot speak in a splendid isolation from the secular marketplace. The loss of depth dimensions of meaning is symptomatic within the church and even if theology can draw imaginative insights from historical achievements it must still shape those insights so they can be heard in a predominantly secular world inside and outside of the church.

The voice crying in the wilderness has been muffled, and proclamation has been transformed into a complaint about the emptiness of everyday life. An intimation of depth is contained in the inverse insight that the surface of experience is not satisfying. A poignant expression of this discontent with surface experience has been the defensive retreat into insanity and the fashioning of pathological containers for the life of the soul. The injuries are too complex, the wounds are too deep, and the silence is too frightening for us to divert our attention from this call for meaning sounded within our culture. The touch of madness is a paradigmatic expression of the afflicted psyche wandering through a shallow world of conventional understanding.[1]

This disfigured hermeneutic of pathological voices is an opening of an eye that sees through a wound, and that eye has been partially accounted for in this century. It is a beginning for our reflections, for in our modern age the charting of depths in the soul began in consulting rooms and asylums when the question of what really goes on in the lives of the mentally ill was seriously posed. The excavation of meaning in the ruins of human lives unearthed stories that resembled mythological tales and called forth further explorations of the imaginal world inhabited by Oedipus, Jesus, unicorns, and classical deities.

A new genre was needed for telling the stories gleaned from the symptoms, dreams, and fantasies revealed in the suffering of neurotic and psychotic patients. A collaborative fiction emerged from the recesses of abnormality that had all the fascination of a well-told mystery with an intricate plot. Freud was the first accomplished storyteller to develop and use this new genre. His

---

[1]The image of "A Touch of Madness" is from a poem of that title in Anna Winquist's *Funerals and Other Celebrations* (Chico, California: New Horizons Press, 1976), p. 37.

development of psychoanalysis provided a needed crucible for the alchemy of the imagination. The ingredients of fragmented lives could be re-collected in the narrative integration of a case history. The excitement surrounding Freud's and Breuer's discovery of a "talking cure" was more than the recognition that hysterical misery can be transformed into common unhappiness; it was a recognition that trifles or commonplace occurrences signal the existence of deeper meanings.[2] Revealing the complicity of conscious experience with unconscious intentions liberated the surface of experience from oppressive trivialization. The reflective spirit had been released from the confines of a narrow definition of empirical thought. Freud's fundamental hypothesis of psychic determinism was a heuristic structure of a new radically empirical method. Nothing could escape the question of meaning. The problem for Freud was to create a structure for the telling of meaning that was as comprehensive as the methodological demand he had accepted as a fundamental hypothesis.

He created a fictional form that allowed him to plot the question of meaning throughout transformations in personal lives. "Telling us *why* is Freud's main aim with his case histories. All his narrative skills are assembled only for the sake of plot."[3] It was his ability to plot that saved the phenomena of experience from perishing in the obscurity of an unintelligible residue. He was able to weave the aberrations of neurotic experiences and psychological fantasies into a meaningful story that had its denouement in the relief of suffering and in the intensification of consciousness. The recurrence of a single plot and its reductive causal schema made it appear that psychoanalysis was an unmasking of experience rather than a collaborative creation of meaning. This is simply a literalistic misconception of the psychoanalytic process that does not account for the subjective structure in understanding.

Freud is a modern precursor to the extensive theological interest in storytelling, theopoesis, narrative, and parable. The collaborative fictions of Freud are a primary reference for plotting in practical hermeneutics. We can ignore the atrophy of psychoanalysis in psychiatric literalism and still learn from Freud, a man of letters. Our dissatisfaction with Freud is that his plotting is not sufficiently complex. "We fail to fall for it [Freud's theory] not because it empirically fails as a hypothesis about human nature, but because it fails poetically, as deep enough, embracing enough,

---

[2]Josef Breuer and Sigmund Freud, *Studies on Hysteria* (New York: Basic Books, 1957), p. 305.
[3]James Hillman, "The Fiction of Case History: A Round," in *Religion As Story*, ed. James B. Wiggins (New York: Harper Forum Book, 1975), p. 130.

esthetic enough plot for providing dynamic coherence and meaning to the dispersed narratives of our lives."[4] However, practical hermeneutics can be no less demanding and rigorous as it complexifies the plotting of a personal story. If practical hermeneutics becomes inflated with archetypal possibilities and ignores the complexity of immediate experience, it blunts the force of narrative and becomes a sophisticated defense of ego-consciousness. Our work can be no less compromising than Freud's in its commitment to the reality of experience and its detailed exposition.

In a letter to his friend, Pastor Oskar Pfister, Freud refused to accept the discretion of an analysis that hesitates before the detailed truth of experience. "Your analysis suffers from the hereditary weakness of virtue. It is the work of an over-decent man who feels himself obliged to be discreet. Now these psychoanalytic matters need a full exposition to make them comprehensible, just as an actual analysis can proceed only when one descends to the small details from the abstractions that cover them. Discretion is thus incompatible with a good presentation of psychoanalysis. One has to become a bad fellow, transcend the rules, sacrifice oneself, betray and behave like the artist who buys paints with his wife's household money, or burns the furniture to warm the room for his model. Without some such criminality there is no real achievement."[5]

The concept of a collaborative fiction in interpretive analysis does not mean a flight from reality. It is instead an acknowledgment of a deep poetic structure in the transformation of events into experience. It is a way of descent to the meaning of small details in the texture of mind. Without the work of the imagination in the interpretation of experience the first collection of a personal history "may be compared to an unnavigable river whose stream is at one moment choked by masses of rock and at another divided and lost among shallows and sandbanks."[6] The enigmatic multiple meanings of symptoms and symbols refer to fantasies that fictionalize the flow of experience in its basic manifestations. We live a fiction prior to any interpretive analysis. Analytical interpretation seeks the intelligibility of the primary experience and consequently adds to that experience through the increment of consciousness. We fantasize the symptom or symbol forward to the

---

[4]*Ibid.*, p. 132.
[5]Ernest Jones, *The Life and Work of Sigmund Freud*, edited and abridged by Lionel Trilling and Steven Marcus (New York: Basic Books, 1961), p. 319.
[6]Sigmund Freud, *Dora: An Analysis of a Case of Hysteria* (New York: Collier Books, 1963), p. 30.

story that it implies. This is the connection that is its primary meaning in experience. Literal interpretation denies the texture of mind and substitutes an abstract pattern of meaning for the flow of experience.

The peculiar genius of psychoanalysis is that it is an exegetical discipline and not an observational science.[7] It makes room for the imagination by beginning with the believed fictions of personal histories and converting these fantasies of meaning through the elaborations of a semantics of desire. Psychoanalysis places the language of symptom and symbol in a state of emergence. We must allow the disclosure of meaning to occur that is already at hand in the enigma of the symbol. If psychoanalysis fails, it fails because it cannot house the multiple meanings announced in the imaginative expansion of the symbolic voice. This, of course, does not deny the utility of psychoanalytically oriented therapies in common psychiatric practice. It simply means that the discovery of a wound on the surface of ego consciousness is an opening and not a closure of our inquiry. As long as language is in a state of emergence, any closure is premature. The re-presentation of experience through interpretation has its own status as a presentation of meaning and continues to hold language in a state of emergence.

The claim that language is in a state of emergence is equivalent to the claim that language conjoins and contrasts imaginative possibilities with the specific determination of fact. The conjunction is dynamic and the contrast is the foundation for new consciousness. That is, language is a matrix of future consciousness as well as a present achievement of consciousness. The care for words is a care for the imagination and the reality of experience that is engendered by placing a monocular vision of the surface against the rich background of multiple possibilities. The rhetoric of an interpretive analysis must be appropriately complex to both express the hearing of a story and facilitate the telling of a story. Interpretation exists in the tension between actuality and possibility. This is how consciousness issues forth into consciousness. Interpretation is both the stuff of consciousness and its self-transcendence. If the plotting of a story is too simple, consciousness replicates itself and there is no advance of understanding. Contrast is diminished and consciousness dims.

Interpretive Analysis

Interpretive analysis is the work of practical hermeneutics in the context of pastoral counseling. It is here that a personal story is

[7]Cf. Paul Ricoeur, *Freud and Philosophy: An Essay on Interpretation* (New Haven: Yale University Press, 1970), pp. 358–75.

re-collected, intensified, and transformed. It is also here that a story can be skewed, distorted, or disguised by the overt or hidden agenda of the pastor. Therefore, it is very important that we discuss principles of interpretation and note some of the problems in the deep collaborative analysis of a story.

The concept of interpretive analysis is a revision of the meaning of pastoral care. We care for the meaning and importance of individual life in the context of the deeper vision of reality that constitutes the significance of calling and conversion. Analysis is interpretive because we recognize the power of the word-event in our own symbolic transformation of consciousness. Interpretation is a natural exigency that proceeds from the presence of the symbol. It is an expression of care for the integrity of both the speaker and the hearer of the word.

Analysis is a movement within the process of interpretation. It is not a concept that can be restricted to the protected professional domains of psychoanalysts or analytical psychologists. Its root meaning is a loosening (*lysis*) throughout (*ana*). It is experience that demands analysis. The "loosening throughout" is prerequisite to hearing the multiple voices of reality constituted in the symbol that makes interpretation possible. Narrow definitions of analysis violate the richness of experience by paradoxically "tightening throughout" the meaning of narrative integration. The authenticity of any analytical method is tested by its disappearance in the deepening consciousness of experience itself.

There are three distinguishable movements in interpretive analysis and narrative integration. First, there is the establishment of a relationship of trust, confidentiality, and collaboration. Second, there are the processes of collection and re-collection of a story. Third, there is a termination of the analytical situation through the cancelling out of interpretive concepts and the personal appropriation of meaning.

There are no techniques that can be simply adopted to establish a relationship of trust for use in practical hermeneutics and interpretive analysis. The establishment of the relationship depends upon the "personal equation" or the depth of the story of the analyst.[8] There must be assurance that chords of meaning can be sympathetically sounded in the telling of a story. This requires a personal appropriation of meaning that suggests images of the wounded physician and the priesthood of the suffering. The concept of a collaborative fiction can be no more profound than the capacities of the pastor or the parishioner. It would be a

[8]James Hillman, *The Myth of Analysis* (Evanston: Northwestern University Press, 1972), p. 14.

particular disappointment if the story were truncated by the inability of the analyst to enter into deep waters of experience. It is to be expected that the level of storytelling will be determined by the capacity for experience of the parishioner. Interpretive analysis is the vessel for the imaginative expansion of experience, although it can also contribute to the depth of the experience and is itself an increment of experience.

Interpretive analysis is not always appropriate in counseling situations that appear within a modern ministry. Sometimes a minister is the first line of encounter for personal and social problems that require short-term intervention or are more appropriate for medical care. Practical hermeneutics recognizes that pathological expressions are often a disguised and distorted grasp for meaning, but we must be sensitive to the limitations of any interpretive model. For example, the somatic correlates of some pathological patterns require the care of a physician and not a priest. It would also be inappropriate to expect someone to commit themselves to intense self-reflection when they are being seriously threatened by outside forces or when they are only trying to gain a perspective on an immediate problem in their families or jobs. Interpretive analysis is primarily a response to the question of meaning in life. This may be an articulate question or it may be expressed symptomatically. When this question is deeply buried in the flow of life and not pressing for recognition, it would be difficult to establish the necessary relationship for serious collaboration. If the symbol does not give rise to thought, the timing is inappropriate. It would be foolish to force or coerce someone into an interpretive context.

To establish a working relationship it is important to explicate basic concepts and to define goals. The practical implementation of hermeneutical understanding requires a considerable commitment of effort. Some of the basic concepts are intellectually demanding, and their personal appropriation can also be emotionally demanding. The promise of practical hermeneutics is that the telling of a story can lead to the discovery of a more satisfying story. The intensification of consciousness and the attendant increment of spirit give density and importance to the fabric of everyday life. The choice of interpretive analysis is a wager for meaning. It is a recognition that the richness of our mythic-symbolic inheritance can be meaningfully integrated into personal life. The re-visioning of the ministerial agenda in practical hermeneutics is not limited to individual counseling, but interpretive analysis is one beginning for an ongoing process of self-understanding. It is not an end in itself. The termination of working sessions can occur when a deeper sense of personal narrative has been achieved and there is an appropriation of necessary conceptual tools for independently continuing the process. Interpretive analysis is a particularly helpful beginning if self-understanding has been obscured by the overlay of many adaptive psychological patterns so that it is difficult for people to assess the applicability of interpretive insights in their lives.

There must not be any false promise in the claims of practical hermeneutics. The analyst should briefly explain the basic concepts that we explored in the first two chapters of this book. The value of narrative and storytelling can be examined together. Narrative is an integrational form that houses patterns of personal and archetypal significance. The parishioner must understand that overinterpretation is a response to the overdetermination of meaning in the symbols of a narrative. Overinterpretation avoids the problems of literalism and naive closure in self-understanding. This is important because many people seek resolution of their anxieties in literalistic closure on open questions. It is also important for someone beginning analysis to realize that the loss of religio-symbolic language is experienced as a psychological aporia. This feeling of hesitating before reality is not a psychological abnormality. Without vessels for the imagination we are all blocked and frustrated in our quest for meaning. The concept of archetypal patterns of meaning is difficult to explain briefly and will probably be amply illustrated in the working sessions through the mediation of symbolic meaning.

The level on which these basic theoretical concepts can be explicated will depend upon the sophistication of the parishioner. The beginning is a point of orientation and the establishment of trust. Interpretive analysis is not the shaman's doorway. The minister must avoid the temptation to masquerade as a magician. A care for persons must coincide with the care for meaning, fantasy, and the imagination.

There is no clear temporal demarcation separating the introductory exploration of basic concepts and the processes of collection and re-collection. The basic interpretive concepts often have to be illustrated in the search for narrative experience before they can be understood and trust in the process is secured. It is equally difficult to differentiate clearly the processes of collection and re-collection or to separate them temporally.

The process of collection always starts in the middle of experience. There is no other existential beginning. We must begin with who we are by virtue of recognizable experiences, tangible feelings, and active fantasies. The symbols that announce themselves in the middle presage the story that is to be told. They are very important because they contain a thread of the story on a variety of levels. The beginning of the narrative must be sought and will become an achievement of interpretive consciousness. The search for origins in storytelling is analogous to the search for foundations in philosophical thinking. They are variations of the commitment to deep analysis. We might say that the search for origins in diachronic patterns of analyses gives density to the parallel search for foundations in synchronic analyses. The ambiguous collision and resultant complementarity of philosophical and psychological interpretations are anticipated in the general theory of language functioning that lies below the concept of practical hermeneutics. The historical immediacy to the privilege of consciousness points to its own structural foundations, but the content of that consciousness reaches toward its temporal origination in the envisagement of possibilities that establish the contrasts necessary for this intensification and penetration. Consciousness can see through itself to its foundation. This is the primary reference to the intelligibility of self-transcendence. It can be immediate and existential. The telling of a story and the search for origins are mediating structures that are satisfied in this self-transcendent achievement of understanding.

Since we must begin in the middle we must carefully watch for those symbolic expressions that get us underway toward interpretation. Freud suggested that "it usually happens that the very recollection to which the patient gives precedence, that he relates first, with which he introduces his confession, proves to be the most important, the very one that holds the key to his mental life."[9] First memories, first dreams, and first fantasies need to be carefully noted. This is the beginning of interpretation from the middle and is a natural orientation to the untold story.

The collection of events, symptoms, dreams, fictions, and fantasies is a repository on the surface that can give way to a downward thinking and carry us to a deeper level of meaning. The key to this process is that the determinateness of fictive events is surrounded by a potentiality for the specific determination of fact. The possibilities that constitute this potentiality are determinative of meaning on different planes of reference or represent that shadow of what could have been. New consciousness emerges in their conjunction with the actuality of experience if that conjunction creates a contrast that is vivid enough to cross the threshold of awareness. In this sense analytical interpretation is the entertainment of new possibilities in the matrix of actual experience for the achievement of expanded consciousness. Such is the odyssey of the imaginative ego.

[9] Sigmund Freud, *Collected Papers, Vol. IV* (London: The Hogarth Press, 1925), p. 359.

Re-collection begins when we render indeterminate the surface collection of events, symptoms, and fantasies. This unraveling of the fabric of consciousness creates a passageway to deeper levels of relational patterns. The destruction at the beginning of re-collection is a familiar mythological theme that can be recognized in myths of origin and renewal, foundational analysis in philosophy, and the more obscure literature of arcane sciences such as alchemy. For example, in alchemy we have vivid images of destruction as a fundamental part of the transformative process. Putrefaction is a necessary part of the alchemical opus. This is paralleled in mythology by reverence for the scarab (a symbol of rebirth, bred and fed in dung), by the numerous accounts of resuscitation following dismemberment, or by the creative and destructive powers of chthonic and phallic divinities in Eastern and Western traditions. The waters of nourishment and renewal are the same as the waters of dissolution. This ambiguity is the shadow of the contrast necessary for the constitution of consciousness that attends the re-collection of experience.

The discontent with the surface of experience is one of the motivations for seeking pastoral counseling. However, sometimes it is the symptomatic fragmentation of the surface that creates the sense of dis-ease that motivates the search for counseling. In both instances we need to fashion tools for downward thinking that reaches toward a more satisfying level of experience. This movement of thought beyond the immediacy of experience is a self-transcendent achievement.

The key to the movement is the ability to render the immediacy of the experience indeterminate and thus open oneself to the ingression of new possibilities. Indetermination is a direct function of the violence of a question. "To ask a question means to bring into the open. The openness of what is in question consists in the fact that the answer is not settled. . . . The sense of every question is realized in passing through this state of indeterminacy, in which it becomes an open question." [10] To question the meaning of surface experience is to anticipate connections with larger patterns of meaning that are indeterminate at the time of questioning. Questioning is a heuristic tool that advances into the openness of possibility. The sense of the question is the knowledge that is contained in the asking of the question. We could not ask a question if we did not sense the presence of a more expansive pattern for interpretation. When we ask a question, we are trying to place experience in this larger context of meaning. The matrix of

[10]Hans Georg Gadamer, *Truth and Method* (New York: Seabury Press, 1975), pp. 326–27.

the question is the surplus of meaning that remains unintelligible in the constricted domain of surface understanding. Concepts such as surface, shallowness, and fragmentation are possible only if they exist in tension with concepts such as depth and wholeness. Raising a question is an explicit grasp toward the intelligibility of the ground evidenced in the conscious contrast on the surface. What we are recognizing is that, in order to constitute itself, experience implicitly houses the structure of the question.

Asking a question is an act of interpretation. It is a fundamental movement of thought by which the specific presentment of images and symptoms is challenged by the possibilities for re-presentation in a larger complex of meaning. In actual practice, the barren force of the question is integrated into a dialogue that accepts experience, moves around it exploring the neighborhood of fantasies and images, and holds the experience against the horizon of our vision. Questions appear in the midst of this process. The discovery of questions implicit in the experience is the advancement of interpretation and the downward shifting of the dialogue. The symbol has delivered its message in the formulation of the question. We become increasingly conscious of the meaning of the symbol in the interpretive resolution of the question. The subsequent mediation of meaning is a further expansion of the imagination.

The act of questioning is reflexive. The questioner becomes the one who is questioned. That is, the resolution of meaning involves the questioner as much as the explicit object of the question. The duality of meaning in the referential significance of the act of questioning loosens the literalism of experience. Questioning can transform the opacity of disjointed voices of the mundane into the transluscence of a symbolic announcement of the extraordinary. We can then fantasize the symbol forward to the story it implies. Thus, interpretation discovers what is at hand in the fullness of experience. It constellates the possibilities that surround specific actualities into patterns that are relevant for an expanded determination of meaning.

Questioning is interpretation's heuristic tool for the acceptance of the meaningfulness of specific symptoms and symbols. Methodology is merged with the hope that psychic afflictions and dark voices belong to a larger context of interpretation. Through the wound on the surface, questions anticipate resonances with archetypal patterns of a common drama. We soon learn to recognize familiar mythological figures and archetypal patterns in their personalized disguises whenever we actively question how the specificity of everyday life fits into a larger scheme of things. That is, questioning can alter the context of memory by asking how things look *sub specie aeternitatis*. We then re-collect our individual stories under an enlarged horizon. They look different from a changed perspective.

The substantive material for interpretation is drawn from the successes and conflicts of everyday life, fantasies and dreams, and also active imagining in the analytical process. Success and conflict are sometimes manifested through symbol and symptom. Even if narrative connections are not discernible, events and episodes can be projected on an abstract temporal continuum. In an analogy to dream interpretation, we can look for the latent story behind the manifest story even if it is disguised and disproportionate in its initial appearance. It is the disguise and disproportion that suggest that a coherent pattern of meaning lies on a different plane of interpretation. Following the way of symbols is not, however, a simple unmasking. Moving to a deeper level of understanding requires an imaginative expansion of the experiential context. The content of the enlarged context often includes remembrance of collective stories, mythologies, and images from theological reflection. We witness this expansion even in the restricted domain of psychoanalysis. "The method in which Freud discovered or rediscovered *memoria* proceeds much in the manner of Plato: moving from concretely real and actual events to recollections extending far beyond the life of the personal individual."[11] When Freud carried the personal story into the Oedipal drama, he mythologized the psyche and transposed the determination of meaning onto a different plane of reference from the immediate world of childhood conflict.

The task at hand in a "talking cure" was the achievement of a new kind of consciousness. If we review the basic structure of the privileged moment of consciousness, we find that the most salient feature is the need for foundational contrast. We become conscious only if determinate actualities are contrasted with each other or with indeterminate possibilities. Language is the paradigm of consciousness because of the conjunctive structure of the proposition, but there are many functional analogues to the linguistic proposition. Visual symbols, auditory contrasts, and ritual actions can all house the need for contrast. The establishment of contrast between actual occasions of experience reinforces linear consciousness and does not alter the level of interpretation. The conjunction of actuality with the imaginative realm of possibilities alters the level of interpretation to a mythopoetic plane.

The shift in level is a shift in context. Consciousness of actuality emerges against an imaginal background; but, as we increase our familiarity with the contours of mythopoetic speech, imaginal

[11]Hillman, *The Myth of Analysis*, pp. 169–70.

figures become conscious against the background of actuality. In both instances, there is an increase of consciousness and vivification of the imaginal ego. We are more than the repetition of past occasions because we live in the neighborhood of a collective memory. The disclosure of archetypal dominants in the determination of meaning reveals, through forceful contrasts, the meaning of our individuality.

For example, specific formulations of universal claims are elaborations of possibilities that contrast with the particularity of experience and thereby intensify the consciousness of the particularity of experience. The satisfaction of theological or mythological journeys is existentially confirmed in the intensification of immediate consciousness and secondarily in the express content of systematic formulations or epic tales. The need for systematic enlargement of thinking is a corollary to the need for a language that is sufficiently complex to contain contrast at the foundation of consciousness. We work on our own consciousness by yoking the realm of possibilities with actuality. Interpretive tools are provisional yokes. Sometimes this is a receptive process in which we seek vessels for symbolic expressions that are naturally conjunctive of the actual and the possible. Interpretation needs the tension that is implied in contrast. The emergent consciousness is the passageway to a more satisfying story and even becomes an element within that story.

The unique contribution of the minister in interpretive analysis is familiarity with the terrain on different levels of interpretation. The foreground of a story from the surface of experience must be collected. Re-collection occurs in the collaborative retelling of that story against the collective background of religious and mythological understanding. This, of course, does not imply that all stories are the same. The background provides contrast with the immediacy of experience and enlarges consciousness. The collaborative fiction emerges from the symbolic voice that is already manifest in the surface story. The individual story is historical and unique. The parishioner is neither Oedipus nor Jesus of Nazareth. Archetypal patterns and mythological figures are forces that need to be accounted for in the particularity of experience but are not substitutes or direct interpretations for that experience. We cannot dissolve the dialogical necessity at the base of consciousness into a new mythological or theological literalism. This would be a denial of the symbolic function in language and analogous to living only on the surface of life. The recognition of archetypal themes and the mythological enrichment of language complexifies the plotting of the emergent story but is not a substitute for that story. A way is prepared for the re-collection of experience and the telling of a story that does not violate the integrity of the symbol.

We can summarize the difference between re-collection and collection by noting the two distinguishable movements in re-collection. First, the surface collection of memories and associations is rendered indeterminate by the force of questioning. The vertical reference of the question to deeper layers of meaning is an acceptance of the symbolic voice. The presence of the question alters the context of interpretation. Language is placed in a state of emergence. Second, consciousness is intensified through the contrast of determinate actualities against the realm of indeterminate possibilities referenced in the multiple voices of the symbol. The display of archetypal patterns that relate to symbols or symptoms is an interpretive experiment. These are trial conjunctions. The meaning can only be confirmed in the transparency of emergent consciousness to the reality of experience itself.

The new achievement of consciousness brings audibility to meaning. We are able to tell a story that belongs to us. The interpretive concepts disappear behind the voice of this story. There is a clear parallel between this claim about the appropriation of personal meaning and Gadamer's insight into textual interpretation. He claims that the criterion for truth in interpretation belongs to the text in the context of our experience. "It is their [interpretive concepts] nature to disappear behind what they bring, in interpretation, into speech. Paradoxically, an interpretation is right when it is capable of disappearing in this way."[12] Through interpretation, the text speaks to us. "This process is simply the concretion of the meaning itself."[13] Without eliminating our own concepts in interpretation and the assimilation of meaning, he sees that correct interpretation is a vessel that is transparent to our experience.

Interpretation brings about changes in patterns of significance and imagery. This is what it means to say that we find a story in telling a story. The criterion of adequacy is the truth of experience in the telling of the story. Something has been added by the achievement of a new consciousness. We stand in the world in a new way. The increment is an ontological transformation that justifies talk of an ontological gain. That is, the complexification of consciousness makes us more than we were by expanding our relational pattern to the world. This is to say that we are different at the end of telling a story.

[12]Gadamer, p. 359.
[13]Ibid., p. 359.

"The inherent rhythm of the narrative movement transposes and transforms events, even invents them . . . . Through the telling of events the soul takes random images and happenings and makes them into particular lived experiences."[14] The advance in concrete experience from disjunction to conjunction is an ontological gain. From the often quoted statement of Alfred North Whitehead, we can again say that "the many become one, and are increased by one."[15] The consciousness emergent in the telling of the story bears witness to this increase by one. We are no longer the same, and this is the primary reference for the achievement of depth in the telling of a story.

The personal narrative or collaborative fiction of practical hermeneutics brings something into being that had not existed before. The alteration of patterns of significance in the re-collection of experience adds to the self-definitional complexity of our being-in-the-world. The self transcends its immediacy. We are simply more than we were before. There is a direct experiential correspondence between this claim and our earlier definition of spirit as a further differentiation of the privilege of consciousness. The collaborative fiction gives visibility to the meaning of spirit. In this sense telling a story is a sacrament of meaning. We jointly labor to transmute the full matter of everyday life into the flowering of spirit that embraces the human soul.

[14]James Hillman, Re-Visioning Psychology (New York: Harper & Row, 1975), p. 143.
[15]Alfred North Whitehead, Process and Reality (New York: Free Press Paperback Edition, 1969), p. 26.

Chapter Four

PERSONAL NARRATIVES

The three personal narratives in this chapter are stories that illustrate the theoretical concept of practical hermeneutics. More importantly they represent a knowledge that comes from praxis, and this knowledge is colored by shades of personality rich in the subtlety of lived experience. Storytelling cannot be abstract. Within the narratives there is a transformation of the interpretive context because narrative development is an internal, interpretive movement. The emergent stories cannot be universalized, but they represent knowledge. A collaborative fiction is a knowledge that comes from praxis and has its place in theology next to theoria.

Portrait I

Reverend James L.

I met the Reverend James L. several years before I interviewed him for this study. James was a retired minister who was articulate and highly respected by his wide circle of church and community friends. Although he had been retired for over ten years, he remained mentally and physically active. When we discussed the possibility for a lengthy interview, he was concerned that his story would be of little interest to others, but I was convinced that the reflective qualities of his ministry and life were important expressions that needed to be revealed. Our conversations were not a journey into unknown possibilities as much as a re-collecting of experiences that had already been heavily weighted with reflective meanings.

After our initial conversations outlining his personal history, it became increasingly clear that the primary agenda of his ministry and the primary definition of his life were as a servant to the needs of the community. He had been a theological liberal and remained a social activist throughout his life. Socially defined human needs gave concrete definition to what was real and important in his understanding of life. It was only at the midpoint of our interviews that I could see that behind the surface of a rich and detailed story of social service was a second agenda that grounded the first level of meaning. The theater of social action not only was significant in itself but also functioned symbolically as an expression of a more personal hidden agenda. The meaning of his ministry was grounded in the hidden agenda. It was here that the self-transcendence sought in the theater of social action became discernible as a real achievement.

James was exceedingly self-critical, and there was a clear discrepancy between his image of himself and his image in the community. He would often talk about himself as failing to measure up to his potential. He quoted from Robert Browning that "the reach is greater than the grasp" and paraphrased this statement by saying that the possibilities for his life were larger than the achievement. He had difficulty reconciling this personal "truth" about his life with the judgment of the community. The discrepancy was real and both perspectives told their own truth. It was, however, the coincidence of meaning and meaninglessness in James's life that was the more profound truth and the subject of this personal history.

James's father was a minister in a protestant church; he described both his mother and father as "positive folk." He had a secure home life in his early childhood as part of a close family. From his earliest memories he recalled exposure to a succession of nationally prominent church and denominational leaders. His father was theologically conservative but not rigid. The atmosphere of his home was "religious" but not characterized by devotional life. Instead, his father would call the family together and read from imaginative literature as well as from scripture. The general boundaries of James's childhood were the home and the church. These boundaries were not fixed. They were transcended by literature in his father's secular devotional readings and later in his own extensive reading of fiction and popular books. The reality of the larger world slowly emerged as real and important to James. The security of childhood allowed him to turn his attention outward without serious conflicts or inner doubts.

His childhood and adolescence appeared uneventful, but there were quiet transformations that deeply influenced the story of his life. He moved three times during his school years when his father was called to new churches. School was easy for him, and he took it for granted in much the same way that he related to the ever-present church. When he was eight years old, he made a confession of faith at an evangelistic meeting but never regarded this as a conversion experience. In fact, there had been no experience in his life that he considered a conversion experience. His religious development was evolutionary and did not visibly interrupt the surface flow of life. His father was not disturbed by modernist currents in theology, and life continued to be a clean, well-lighted place. His home was a nineteenth century world brushed by evangelistic enthusiasm on one hand and dimly aware of theological controversy on the other. The world was main street America; and it was not surprising that, as James turned toward this world with increasing care and understanding, the shape of his ministry and life became pragmatic and social in its definition.

Literature consciously revealed a deeper layer of significance that was to undergird his life on the surface. As a high school student he began to read poetry and drama. In particular he was influenced by Charles Kennedy's *The Servant in the House*. Reading this play was a "spiritual experience" for him. The contrast between an ambitious local bishop and the Bishop of Benares who was disguised as a servant in the house revealed a power and vision of reality that was sought in the expression of James's own life. He thought that this play might have contributed to his first consciousness of a future ministerial vocation. His being a servant in the house was accented with an inexplicable sense of reality. The surface appearance was not a proper determinant of reality. He continued to reach for this deeper vision and in later life had an undeveloped feeling that this vision was also expressed in oriental religious thinking. If he were to be a servant in the house, he needed a context for the expression of his commitment. He claimed that the "muckrakers" in the popular press raised his consciousness of social injustice and political corruption until he was seething in anger. The church seemed to be a place where he could be both a servant and a prophet.

He did not actually make the decision to enter the ministry until he was in college. He was not deeply influenced by any particular college professors; and, like his childhood, this period was primarily characterized by an evolutionary growth in consciousness. Summer jobs as a salesman and later as a newspaper reporter seemed to have a greater influence on him than his classes in college. He wrote to his father that he had decided to enter the ministry because of the poor quality of preaching he had heard while a travelling salesman. It was unsettling to him that he had had neither a conversion experience nor a dramatic call to the ministry. The real significance of these decisions was hidden in the deeper story that he was living, but this was discovered only in retrospect.

James entered the pastorate before his seminary education. His concept of the ministry was educational rather than pastoral. He had become a social liberal and said that the social gospel was more important to him than theology. Both anti-theological and anti-clerical feelings developed during this period of his ministry. Even his understanding of the New Testament was anti-clerical. Because he associated the symbolic function of language with clerical prerogatives, he rejected this tool in the understanding of his ministry. Reality was immediate. "Folks are human beings."

His concept of the ministry and his understanding of persons did not articulately embody his concern with a hidden agenda and allow room for the disguised servant in the house. The symbolic meaning of his work was not evident to consciousness. He thought at this time in his pastorate that part of the problem was that he was not a good denominationalist. He said that he always felt cramped in a church situation. The immediate church situation did not speak of the reality he had glimpsed in his personal quest. With a retrospective vision he realized that even at this stage in his ministry he understood preaching to be more quest than proclamation. On a personal level the fullness of ministry resided in the act and not in the content of the spoken word.

James had planned to resume his education after parish experience but had to wait until he could afford to return to school. He also felt that seminary would be more profitable after he extended his parish experience. He later enrolled in a respected seminary. The direction of his life was not altered in any significant way. He discovered language and categories that could further express the commitments he had already made. Theology made James more conscious of the substance of religious experience, but he thought that theological literature did not have the depth to challenge his sense of reality. Of course, he had never had a clearly defined theological position, although his sympathies were with liberalism and the social gospel movement. He became convinced that reality was located in the expression of an "inner something" through practical social application. The internal vision of reality was not made explicit, but he knew that it was implicated in the social concerns that were tangible and concrete. The language and institution of the church were important if they could facilitate expression of this inner reality. He said, "I believed in the church and the church as an institution, but I was always unhappy by the vast distance between where we were and where we ought to be." At that time he sought unity and ecumenical accord and blamed denominationalism for many of his frustrations. However, the feelings of being "cramped" pointed toward a larger issue that was repeatedly manifested in his life. His life in the church did not provide the language or structure that could mediate his personal, internal vision of reality. "The people in my congregation couldn't understand what I was after." In fact, the "inner reality" remained inarticulate and unthematized for him as well.

James seriously considered leaving the ministry on a variety of occasions when the "cramped" feeling was especially frustrating. His feelings, sympathies, and interests could not be bounded by the institution, but his work was increasingly centered in the maintenance of an institution. He felt that "the real things are the personal things." However, his concept of the personal was not individual. The personal drama was projected onto a social drama. Transformation was understood as social change even though the existential significance of social change was located in the "inner reality" of the individual. There was a disjunction in this formulation that obscured the meaning of his experience. The visible measure of transformation was societal and institutional change, but the importance of what was to be measured was hidden in the agenda of personal growth. The full meaning of his ministry could not be assessed because the yardstick for measurement was inadequate and could not be applied to the hidden agenda. This would even be true if institutional and social change could have been detected. The feeling of being cramped reflected not only the inability to evaluate his experience but also the inability to make a judgment on the inertial qualities of the church. It would be naive to undervalue the importance of social commitments, but the externalization of the inner vision of reality was not sufficiently expressive of what was real and important to him. He saw that his measure was inadequate. He said: "The church has been concerned with social and financial status rather than with what is actually happening in the lives of people. Maybe I can't get a hold of the depth, and that is the major source of frustration."

James stayed with the church and, surprisingly, took a position in denominational administration. The theater for life remained social and institutional. He thought that the formula "faith seeks understanding" implied a more profound agenda, "faith seeks expression." The drama of faith was to be played in the community.

At this point in his ministry he acknowledged that social achievements are always failures when judged against a horizon of possibilities. He affirmed, however, that one could become conscious of oneself and of one's purpose in social action. He believed that if you put your hand to a plow you discovered your hand as well as the plow. Even if you did not cut furrows in the earth you still discovered your hand. The hidden agenda of self-understanding was clearly manifested in these reflections.

James tried not to think of executive work in institutional terms. He was a pastor to pastors and to all of the churches in the state. This expanding sphere of influence did not eliminate his feeling of being cramped. While an administrator, he felt separated from church people and from what he had thought was most important in the ministry. After many years in executive work he decided to complete his ministry in the pastorate. His return to the pastorate was actually for only four years. He then returned to executive work but this time in an interdenominational position. When he was in the pastorate, he made a shift toward pastoral visitation and personal contact. This shift was actually a response to community needs, not personal needs. The transformation was consistent with his general concept of a socially oriented ministry. His later work in an ecumenical council was not importantly different from his work in the denomination. He was still limited and felt cramped.

I asked him if he still felt cramped after over ten years of retirement. "In some senses I do. Do we ever not feel cramped? I seem to be confined to an area where my influence is so minimal. I see the possibilities, but I haven't found the community where there is a whole-hearted commitment to the attainment of possibilities. . . . We can't get a hold of what is most important but neither can we leave it alone."

Liberal theology and the social gospel were companions for James throughout his ministry. They did not fail to give him direction and deepen his sense of reality. However, now, as he enters into advanced old age, an important transformation is occurring. He now says that "seeing beyond comes with age. It is increasingly difficult to verbalize. My concern was with what can happen in human society, but we are terribly poverty stricken if there isn't something that reaches beyond possibilities of attainment." A theological shift is present in this statement. He has not abandoned—nor should he—his liberal theological categories, but he does realize that we are not satisfied unless we see beyond the immediate. There comes a time when we must be able to talk about the limits of life as authentic human experiences. We must be able to talk about death and beyond to complete the telling of our story.

After reviewing his personal history, our working sessions turned to the question of the meaning of life. These sessions were instructive to me and provided the opportunity for James to evaluate the reach of his theological categories. There was a very real sense in which he felt that he had not succeeded in his ministry. The societal and institutional transformations that he sought were not realized. It was this feeling that had made him hesitate when I first requested that we talk about his life. The immensity and weight of social problems were no less real at the close of his ministry than at the beginning. He touched many individuals in his life, but the hoped-for changes in church and society still existed only as possibilities luring him into the future. The gap between promise and fulfillment was an inevitable judgment on the program he defined for his life. However, the depth that he experienced in the gap gave meaning that transcended his immediate goals. He was able to recognize human needs and sort out trivial from important experiences. He had a language that allowed him to talk about what was essential in his life, but the categories that he used to interpret experience functioned almost exclusively on the level of immediate social concerns. Limiting questions that ask why social transformations and change are desirable reached beyond the boundaries of his interpretive categories. His liberal theology was not foundational. This does not mean that it did not have depth. It did have depth but was not able to explicate the significance of its own depth. This is not a problem if we affirm the symbolic function of the language of hope and promise. However, James distrusted symbolism because of its association with clerical themes. He was able to talk about what was essential to his humanity but not why it was essential. The relationship to essential themes was abbreviated. The spirit was "cramped" in the narration of his story. I think that he recognized that his interpretive categories were limited to the immediacy of the here and now. This accounts for a romantic fascination with the Orient that persisted throughout his life. He thought that an encounter with Buddhism could give him a perspective on his life.

In fact, his perspective on life had undergone a transformation in later years. He expressed this by saying that the whole concept of the immediate situation was changed by a sense of the on-goingness of life. He was agnostic about the forms of after-life. His beliefs in the persistence of personality and immortality gave him a perspective on the wholeness of his story. "I have no idea of what lies beyond, but I have a feeling of opportunity."

James was close to his wife. Her recent death had a significant impact on his life. She had been ill and a semi-invalid for many years. Her illness changed the social pattern of his life but not his theological perspective. He said, "Illness is a part of life for all of us. I never felt that I was different from anyone else. The immediate experience did not make a difference. Liberal theology can allow us to survive suffering." After her death he allowed himself an image of his wife that was comforting but must be interpreted symbolically. He said, "I realize the utter foolishness of my picture, but I have the strongest conviction that she has entered into some kind of fuller life." The urgency of this image is psychological, but it has theological implications. Theological symbols began to gain in weight and meaning. They announced the weight of possibilities that transcended the immediate situation. The image of his wife was "utterly foolish" only when it was interpreted literally.

The psychological need to formulate a myth about death invested apocalyptic thought with new meaning and pushed Easter to the center of his faith. He said that neo-orthodoxy touched him only as a glancing blow in the formation of his theological understanding, but the stress on the centrality of the Easter-event must be reckoned with in any theology. Christmas used to be the most important holiday because it was a time of family gathering. This was an important part of its meaning. "Now when I think of Christmas, I have to think of Easter and Good Friday." James had lived the symbols of the Christian faith, and after our working sessions they pushed their way above the threshold of consciousness. The reach that exceeds the grasp marks the coincidence of meaning and meaninglessness.

James was unique among the people I interviewed for this study. It is possible that because he was considerably older than most of the people interviewed, he had already made decisions about what was important to tell in his story. He reported his life to me without a serious struggle. I was not actively involved in directing the interview. The familiar shadows of childhood fixations and adolescent crises were not evident. This was a period of philosophical unification and adjustment for James.

Unlike many modern men and women, James did not lack a language to articulate what was real and important to him as he journeyed through life. Perhaps it was because of the security of his childhood and the consequent ability to turn toward the world around him without nagging inner doubts that he could recognize meaning in the struggle for human dignity and social well-being. Society was a complex container that could house and enrich imaginative consciousness. For him, self-consciousness was world-consciousness. His personal story was projected into the church and community.

Now in the later reflective years of James's life it is important that he recognize himself in the story that he continues to live. The social frontier is also a spiritual frontier. Meaning can be added to meaning in the conscious enjoyment of life. This is a ministry that can be directed toward him.

James was a pastor to pastors and a servant in the life of the church. It is easy to overlook the challenge to a contemporary ministry illustrated by his needs because of his service and solid identity with the church. It is a priestly function of the ministry to lift personal struggles into a larger context of meaning. It is also a priestly function of the ministry to illuminate how struggles in larger contexts bring into consciousness the personal meaning of life. The struggle between meaning and meaninglessness can take place on a variety of levels. The creation of consciousness in the coincidence of these levels can be one of the great tasks of an interpretive ministry.

Portrait II

Catherine T.

Catherine T. is a respected lay-leader in a local church community. She is married and the mother of two children, one married and the other a teenager, still living at home at the time of our discussions. Catherine willingly agreed to my request for a series of interviews because of her increasing interest in theological understanding. There was no evidence of a psychological urgency to religious questions when we began the interview process.

The surface of Catherine's life was untroubled, and she was often sought as a counselor by friends who were facing religious or personal problems. The most salient feature of her public personality was her belief that she lived in a "spiritual world" that was more important than the everyday world. Her faith that "our lives are in God's hands" was comforting to her friends even though the content of this affirmation was shrouded in the mystery of private experience. The interviews challenged the privacy of her experience but were not seen as a challenge to her primary confession of faith. Her secret "spiritual world" had not been meaningfully altered by the journey through her personal story and continued to function as a source of strength and a refuge from the immediacy of everyday concerns. It did, however, become very clear that her sacred language was not descriptive of the "spiritual world" and could not be isolated from the immediate empirical world once she opened herself to the question of its meaning.

The multivalent qualities of symbolic language are well illustrated in Catherine's personal story. The overdetermination of meaning in the function of the symbol is a passageway into new experience. When Catherine allowed herself to listen to the voices of religious language in her "spiritual world," she was soon confronted with the importance of her unique individuality.

This intersection of private and traditional uses of religious language can be untangled and understood only in the context of her personal story. In fact, the story of Catherine T. cannot be told without attention to the multiple uses or functions of religious language in the generation of her self-consciousness. What is of particular interest is that religious language and ideas were used to forestall experience of the immediacy of feelings and yet, in another context, were used to enlarge the reference for the determination of meaning. It was this conjunction of meaning in religious symbols, particularly in the symbol of the Christ, that was experienced not only as a collision of worlds but also as the possibility for a new self-consciousness. By telling her story,

Catherine began to discover a story that was more challenging and more satisfying.

Catherine was born the fifth of six children in a small midwestern town. She remembered her childhood as a time of loneliness and self-doubt. She was close to two of her sisters but felt tormented by her oldest brother. She also felt that her mother didn't like her and that there was nothing she could do to please her. Privately, she resented her mother and also felt guilt for their bad relationship.

Catherine's father was the central figure in her childhood. He was strong and gave the impression that he had come to terms with his own destiny. Catherine felt secure with her father because she thought she was a special child to him. She sensed that her mother and the other children resented the protective relationship she had with him. Catherine's parents were not demonstrative of their feelings. Though she felt close to her father, their relationship was not warm and open. Catherine never shared her deepest feelings and sometimes would go for as long as two weeks without talking unless directly questioned by her parents or school teachers. These periods of silence lasted into her high school years and occasionally still occur.

During her primary school years, Catherine began to feel increasingly isolated from other people. At night she experienced intense feelings of loneliness and what she now recollects as meaninglessness. As sleep approached she was confronted by a whole phantasmagoria of frightening images and thoughts. She questioned the possibility of having lived before as another person or animal. She was comforted by imagining that she had been, or was now, a horse. She would ask: "Why am I thinking these thoughts? Where do they come from?" These thoughts were closely guarded secrets that she could not share with her family. One night, when she was nine or ten years old, she became convinced that she was a bird and at two o'clock in the morning tried to fly out of her second story bedroom window. She was not injured but was scolded by her mother for awakening the household. Her mother did not even ask why she had jumped out of the window. There was no comfort and no understanding. These strong feelings of being overtaken by ideas or images persisted into her high school years as an inarticulate threat to the normality of her life.

The prolonged periods of silence were an inflationary expression of what had become characteristic of Catherine's life. The fearsome images and ideas were drowned in silence. She had no language that could express her experience, and it would have been dangerous to talk about these ideas in the context of her family or small town culture. She was suspect because of her isolation and silence, but this withdrawal protected her from further rejection. She was a good student in school and spent most of her time away from school, studying or reading. When she entered high school, she became involved in church youth organizations. The church fixed the parameters of her social life and opened up what could have been new possibilities for human relationships.

More importantly, the church supplied her with a language and conceptual framework to protect her from night terror. A high school Sunday School teacher stressed the nearness of God and the efficacy of a personal relationship with Him. Catherine was drawn to this man and felt comforted by his ideas. He personalized the Bible, and she became familiar with biblical language. When surrounded by evening shadows she would ward off frightening thoughts and images by reading from the Bible. Her teacher had said that God is inside us and available as our protector. She identified with this mysterious God but not with the Jesus of the New Testament. She said: "Jesus didn't speak to me, but the crying out of David in the Psalms made contact." In particular, it was the language of utter despair, fluctuating with joyous praise, that gave her the first feeling of being understood.

This discovery of a personalized biblical language was both an opening and a closure in her life. For the first time she had a language available to talk about what was most real and important in her experience. The language of David dignified her suffering by raising it into the ultimate context of a holy history. The drama of a lonely, small-town girl filled with self-doubt was transposed onto the stage of God's action. The meaning of her struggle was inflated, and she was comforted by the election to live in God's world. She was also comforted by the escape from the world of immediate human feelings. God's world masked the terrible world of adolescence and closed off a world of personal interaction. However, socialization was skewed by this newly discovered vocation.

The internal world was accented with reality and was the seat of authority for the determination of meaning. The church community's interpretation of the Bible was never a decisive factor in Catherine's understanding. This is well illustrated during her junior year in high school when she witnessed an accident in which one of her friends was killed. He had not been baptised, and she asked her minister if he could be saved. The minister said that he could not. This was so totally unacceptable to Catherine that she altered her college plans to study for a religious vocation in the mission field. The church was not as real as her private religious world, but by distancing herself from traditional church vocations she saw no way of being responsive to the calling she felt with her discovery of the Bible.

Catherine married soon after graduating from high school. Marriage changed the external circumstances of her life, but she continued to live in her private world. Her husband, Ray, was deeply involved in a pentecostal church. After a short stay in the Middle West, they moved to a large western city. The pentecostal experience was frightening to Catherine. She had no family or friends in this new community but tried to make friends in the church even though she was uncomfortable. She withdrew further into herself until she began to experience afresh the night terror that she knew as a child. She described the first years of her marriage as a time of quiet desperation.

She gave birth to her first child in the second year of her marriage and easily made the role shift to wife and mother. What is unique about the first years of Catherine's married life is that the desperation she felt did not seem to be significantly related to her new roles as wife and mother. She seemed to have little trouble making these adjustments. However, the story that she was living at this time was primarily internal. Ray's pentecostalism challenged Catherine's self-understanding. She did not have a well-defined understanding of herself or of religion, and she soon discovered that her private reading of biblical texts collided with fundamentalism. She felt deficient because her religious life was not outwardly emotional and compensated for this lack by exaggerating her inward feelings.

Catherine was suspicious not only of the outward expression of emotion in the church but also of her newly emphasized inward feelings. She vaguely connected the church's emotionalism with sexuality, and this was totally unacceptable to her. This was reinforced by the flirtations of Ray's best friend, a recently divorced ministerial student. Catherine felt uneasy with herself and with him. She declared that "all the high emotionalism in the church isn't for real." The real world was private. She generated internal excitement by returning to her earlier vocation as a child of God. She began to fantasize that she was blessed with extraordinary gifts and could heal with a touch of her hand. This escape into an inflated view of her person was short-lived, but it remains one of the clearest expressions of how she could use religion to mask the world of immediate anxieties. Interestingly, she felt herself estranged from God as she pursued this fantasy of extraordinary closeness to him. A trip to her hometown convinced her that she was in fact living a fantasy. She felt frustration but not desolation. The anger, hurt, loneliness, and hostility toward her mother debunked the fantasy, but it also freed her to examine freshly what she was doing with her life. After returning from the visit with her mother, she dropped out of church for a year. She did not know what she was looking for, but she did know that she was restless and still on a quest. She said, "There was a missing compartment in my life, and I needed a door to enter into it." Catherine shopped for a church so that her daughter could attend Sunday School and settled on a mainline protestant denomination. She felt at home. The internal agenda was not resolved, but she had discovered much needed space in which she could explore new possibilities. She no longer had to defend herself from the emotional claims of the pentecostal experience. The emphasis on the personal Jesus retreated into the background, and she could again be comfortable with the isolated splendor of her private God.

She worked in this church for almost seven years. She respected the minister, and he encouraged her to become involved in activities. This seven years was a time of externalization and socialization. She was less reflective and began to experience a new restlessness that was not directly associated with her new religious life. Catherine began to work nights at a factory to support a new house. She first loved the house and would think, "How can something this beautiful belong to me?" She soon became a slave to the house and also to the demands of the family. The house was slowly transformed into a prison. She became angry and asserted newly discovered feelings about her own identity. In her mind, she was no longer simply identified as Mrs. Ray I. This transformation was internal and found little expression in her expanding social life. She fought with herself to do "fun things" such as playing cards or going to the movies. She would rehearse possibilities but did not actualize her desires. She felt frustrated and unfulfilled.

The gap between desire and satisfaction, the felt lack of fulfillment, is clarified by a repeating dream from this period in Catherine's life. The hidden side of her story was manifested, but it was not deciphered at the time. The importance of this dream illustrates the value of listening to dreams in the development of a narrative, as well as the fact that it gives deeper insight into Catherine's struggle. The recurrence of the dream suggests that, although the message was being delivered, she was not conscious of its meaning.

The manifest content of the dream was fairly simple. In it, Catherine was sitting on a couch admiring her house. The house had been remodeled by removing a wall and building a large planter. Big, beautiful, live plants reached up to the ceiling from this planter. (In fact, Catherine didn't like plants and decorated her home with only a few plastic reproductions of plants.) She was impressed that these were *real* plants and were growing in *real* dirt. Before waking she would think with astonishment and satisfaction: "This is my house."

When Catherine related the dream to me, its meaning was still hidden from her. She had many associations with the seven year period in which the dream repeated itself but remembered the dream only because she had a dream during the previous week that used similar props. She didn't remember exactly when she began to have this dream, but she was twenty-six years old when she entered this period of frustration. She remembered that she was seeking an undefined reality in her life. She repeated: "I needed a door. There was a missing compartment in my life." She did not, however, connect this search for a door to a missing compartment with the removal of a wall in her dream. There was no *real* dirt in her life at this time. She did not nourish new life with the common soil of humanity. The realm of powerful chthonic symbols frightened her, and she again retreated into her spiritual world. In her private moments she would cry and pray. She was familiar with the loneliness of withdrawal and began to value her loneliness as an alternative expression for the depth that she was seeking. The loneliness went too far. She felt rejected by God, and she missed the nebulous satisfaction of her earlier vocation as a "child of God."

She tried to compensate by increased activity in the church and the acceptance of leadership responsibilities. At first she succeeded only in fragmenting her life. The private world remained untouched. Over the passage of several years she began to internalize the satisfaction of her church work but did not resolve the problem of her dream. This was clearly illustrated by a new dream that precipitated a remembrance of the earlier one. The unfinished agenda of the earlier dream was still pressing for conscious recognition in Catherine's life. In the more recent dream the scene was a two-story house. The planter was now on the second floor. Catherine was watering the planter, but in this dream there were no living plants. She thought in the dream: "I am so tired of cleaning up." She then turned to a younger woman and said: "You don't have to pick up after me."

After we talked about the dream, it was clear that Catherine resented the recurrence of problems that she thought she had resolved a long time ago. The house was now multi-leveled, and the younger woman whom she associatively identified as herself had come up the stairs from a lower floor. The planter was no longer flowering on the lower floors of the unconscious but was now in the living room of consciousness. There were, however, no plants and no real dirt. The emptiness of the planter and the pressing intrusion of the younger self were the immediate problems for Catherine. She felt the need to water the planter but was not yet ready to accept the possibility for the presence of real dirt and real plants that were associated with the dreams of the younger self. The container or vessel for life had been moved into consciousness, but plants must be rooted in the earth, and the container remained empty. Catherine needed to recognize the significance of the container outside of this particular dream image.

The dream had an impact on the interview process. The simple progression of the narrative telling of Catherine's story was now constantly interrupted by the need to explore chains of associative thoughts. The image of the empty planter produced anxiety and there was an urgent pressing for some type of resolution. New feelings, images, and associations became the main topic of conversation. Catherine had the distinct feeling that "something was going on" and mentioned it to her close friends. She explored biblical and light devotional readings in a bid for understanding. This was consistent with her life during the past six years. She described her experience as alternating between "highs" and "valleys." During the highs she felt in touch with God but not with herself. She described the experience as follows: "I am not really there—I am not me. Someone else is in complete control." She would think, "I don't have to express feelings . . . the spirit translates feelings." She wanted to do good works because she thought they would anchor her feelings and give her something to grasp. However, the good works were never the occasion for the feelings she valued so highly. The spiritual world remained disembodied and disconnected from everyday life. She stated that the feelings accompanying her spiritual experiences were unreal but, at the same time, more real than anything else in her life. She tried to protect the integrity of her experiences through a variety of paradoxical expressions and felt that if she shared her experiences she was in danger of losing them.

Juxtaposed with her statement about the unwillingness to share her experience was a confession that she was worried. She realized that, although she had a knowledge of God, she did not know Jesus. Both the positioning and the intensity of this confession signaled that she was telling me something important. Perhaps we had discovered a clue to the conscious correlate for the empty planter in her dream thoughts. The talk of Jesus, so thoroughly interwoven in the fabric of her devotional life, was empty of experiential significance. "I know what he was, but Jesus is still out there. Jesus is not mine, and I cannot use personal terms when I talk about him."

Catherine said that she told some of her friends at church about her inability to relate to Jesus, and they found her confession incomprehensible. She could not understand their easy familiarity in talk of Jesus, but it was very clear to me that she was both more sophisticated theologically and more familiar with the New Testament than her friends. The psychological force of the dogmatic formulation for the Christ, as fully God and fully human, was very real to her. The incarnational motif was constantly announced in her favorite Bible stories. She could readily accept that Jesus as the Christ was fully God. It was the humanity of Jesus that caused her anxiety. Her friends casually accepted a docetic Christ, but Catherine had become too conversant with theological tradition not to notice the discrepancy between their solution and her confession of faith. The symbol of the Christ had become so heavily constellated with personal energy that she could not ignore its voice without a sense of deep personal loss.

The symbolic coincidence of man and God in the Christ-event is usually celebrated because it announces the availability of God's love. For Catherine, the primary significance of this symbol was its humanizing power. She felt excluded from a personal relationship with the Christ because she could not acknowledge her humanity in a relationship to the human voice of the symbol.

I asked her to talk about the fully human Jesus, and she resisted my suggestion. We constructed an imaginary scene in which she met the man, Jesus of Nazareth. She wanted Jesus to be sitting on a level higher than herself. When I suggested Jesus might touch her, she flatly declared: "You can't have that part of my life." The reference for the "you" remained ambiguous, but "that part of my life" referred to "family, self, and deeper me." She then declared that the spiritual part of life is safer.

After further conversation it became clear that Catherine did not want to talk about the humanity of the Christ because she did not want to examine her own humanness. She said, "I am afraid of losing control of my feelings." Anger was the feeling that was most available to her, but it was her sexuality that was most frightening. In another strange juxtaposition of statements she said: "I cannot talk about humanity. Sex is a dirty word." Humanization became identified with vulnerability, frailty, and sexuality.

Catherine acknowledged a desire to get in touch with herself, but this was secondary to her desire to be in touch with God. The coincidence of the divine and the human in the symbolism of the Christ was a stumbling block. At first, she argued that a denial of gender in human relationships allowed for a deeper love that was Christ-like. She wasn't convinced by her own argument.

She then said that it was safer not to look at herself as a woman. "I do not want to be attractive to men. . . . I feel comfortable when I deny gender." In fact, she did not feel comfortable about the denial of her own sexuality. She said, "I feel all of the events in my life are pushing me to be a whole person. To be a woman is to feel lovely, clear like a creek."

This was a hard time for Catherine. She was confused by inconsistencies in her own thinking. She felt that she was in the middle of a personal and religious quest and was excited by the immediacy of her struggle. This was evidenced by her comment, "I have a real sense of living through part of my story now—the story is quite dark, but I am not afraid."

Catherine's identification of humanization with the recognition of sexual feelings explains her inability to approach a fully human Jesus. The world of sexuality was dangerous. Her mother had taught her not to talk seriously with boys, and she had not developed a language of intimacy that allowed her to articulate and situate sexual feelings in the larger context of her life. "Sex is a dirty word" and there was no *real* dirt in the living room of her consciousness. Even as a child, when she imagined herself to be a horse, she was afraid of the power of these thoughts. "Why am I thinking these thoughts?" Of course, she was not conscious that the horse is often a libidinal symbol. Religion was a retreat and a tool of repression in her childhood that enabled her to escape from these unwanted feelings. Now, at the center of her religious experience, she was forced to encounter the power of immediate feelings.

Catherine had experienced a loss in her life that remained unnamed until we began the interviews. The full humanity of the Christ functioned analogously in her conscious understanding with the images of real dirt and real plants in her dream life. The disembodiment of spiritual life was now acknowledged as a loss of feelings and a distortion of experience. She desired warmth and intimacy in human relationships but did not identify her needs with sensuality or sexuality. In fact, she did not accept my analysis of a sexual aetiology of the psychological repression that restricted and distorted humanizing tendencies in her life. She thought that she would lose more than she would gain by allowing sexual feelings to enter the arena of conscious experience and be integrated with her concept of womanhood. Of course, this conspiracy of consciousness, with existing unconscious resistances, contributed to her inability to account for the range of lost feeling and experience caused by the repression. The wound suffered by consciousness is not limited to explicitly sexual feelings but is extended to experiential derivatives and associational ideas. It is around the fringes of this gaping hole that Catherine noted the loss of meaning that frustrated her ability to embrace a fully human Jesus.

Catherine was not totally successful in the repression of sexual feelings. She related sexual fears to early childhood fears of being overtaken by feelings that were not easily controlled. She indicated a preference for seeing herself as a child of God, rather than as a woman. However, she had become too conscious of living through a story to deny that a struggle was occurring within her life. The personal narrative was unresolved, but the continuing struggle for meaning, much of it unconscious, had received a sanction in consciousness.

Catherine had become very aware of working on the fringes of repressed feeling. It was the Christ-symbol that drew her consciousness into the center of the individuation process. The importance of narrative interpretation was that she identified the power of this symbol with the passage of her life. The same religious language that had been used to mask feelings was now used for disclosure. Through interpretation, Catherine had become a hearer of the word. We terminated our working sessions without a sense of closure. Catherine was confident that her story was personally significant and that she had acquired some skills that she could use in an ongoing interpretation of experience.

Eight months later, I visited Catherine to talk with her about our sessions. She had worked very hard to allow experience to have a conscious voice and announce new meanings to her. She said, "I don't think that most of us realize we have a story. It has made a difference. I had always looked at myself as dull and colorless. This is not true now. I experience enthusiasm about everyday life."

Catherine had been ill and had undergone a forced convalescence. She said that her frailty became public and that now she could admit people into her private world. Her whole family had become benefactors of her self-valuation. She no longer lived in retreat. Of particular significance for her was a newly discovered ability to talk with her mother. In general, she said, "I can enjoy people again."

There is no conclusion to this personal narrative. Catherine has entered into a new phase of her life—one she can enjoy more fully since it is enriched by reflection and increased understanding. In my most recent interview with her, she said that now, during difficult times, she sits down and asks, "What is this saying to me? Am I opening doors or am I in a waiting period?" Reassured by her sense of the meaningfulness of the struggle and by her belief that "God is taking care of me," she allows central symbols of her experience to give rise to thought. This has provided an added dimension and depth to her life that does not deny the immediacy of feelings but contributes to a contrast at the foundation of consciousness.

Catherine was pleased to report that she could now relate to the concept of a fully human Jesus. She could value her womanhood without giving up her private spiritual world entirely; it is still a refuge and possesses comfortable familiarity. Although she can relate to a human Jesus and to a fully divine Christ, the psychological coincidence implied by the symbolic coincidence in dogmatic formulations of the Christ has not been achieved. What is exciting is that she is conscious of the lure toward wholeness.

The portrait of Catherine T. is complex and challenges simplistic adaptations of secular models for psychotherapy in pastoral counseling. Catherine was psychologically responsive to a theology of proclamation. The symbol gave rise to thought, and the unexpected psychological inversion of what is usually thought to be the power of Christological symbolism is a theme that deserves understanding in the contemporary church. The church has been a repository of powerful transformational symbols. Practical hermeneutics is a recognition of this inheritance.

Portrait III

Wanda D.

The promise of practical hermeneutics is that to tell a story on one level can help us to discover and enter into a story on a more satisfying level. The privilege of consciousness is extended by attending to the multiple voices of already conscious symbols. The expansion of consciousness is possible only when the fixed meaning of symbols on one level of interpretation is questioned and conjoined with other possibilities for meaning. This process establishes necessary contrasts at the foundation of an expanding consciousness. However, without an integrative vision of the process of storytelling the overdetermination of meaning in symbols can be experienced as an indeterminateness of meaning that threatens fragile achievements of self-understanding. This experience can lead to a loss of confidence and a desire to narrow the neighborhood where we live to safe and familiar territory. A choice is made, consciously or unconsciously, to surrender the promise of an expanded world of meaning for security and unity on the surface of understanding. It may be that the time is not right to risk the stability of surface understanding because of environmental pressures, or it may be that the shadow of repressed feelings intertwined with the exploration of a not yet conscious story generates anxieties that paralyze the force of inquiry.

The story of Wanda D. is exemplary of a narrowing circle of consciousness that has temporary resolution in the peace of an uneasy suppression of the questioning spirit. Wanda initiated the interview process with a confession that her story had lost its plot and that life was generally experienced as closed in a stalemate. She was in her middle forties and felt a nostalgic desire to be younger and stronger. She said that she had always been quiet and repressive but that now she was disappointed in marriage, shattered by her children, and victimized by failing health. Wanda's world seldom crossed the boundaries of family life. Her personal story had been subsumed under the drama of family life as both a child and an adult. She basically felt that identity is conferred on a person by others. She uncritically adapted to roles defined by her family and a conservative community. By conventional definition she was a good daughter, good wife, and good mother. That is, she did not violate the rules or transgress the expectations of family or church (the most visible social institutions in her life). The nebulous promise of a "good" life was not fulfilled and, when I interviewed her, she was angry. Until now she had swallowed her disappointment and anger and was regularly treated for stomach disorders. She felt that now was a time "to get on with living" and wanted to talk about her life.

Wanda had difficulty articulating what was real and important in her life. There were no conscious criteria that she used to test the reality of her experience. Meaning and value were flattened in an objective representation that eluded subjective enjoyment. Wanda did say that "breathing deeply is symbolic of feeling good." Wanda wanted to feel good and to her this meant inner peace and calm, "breathing deeply," and family affirmation. She said, "I hate for people to create waves. I don't want to be a person who runs free and wild." Wanda told me a factual account of her life. She had very little access to the imaginative world of fantasy and dreams. When we explored the question of meaning, I created waves and we terminated the interviews. It was clear to me that the fear of "running free and wild" was a part of the fantasy world that was so little expressed in our working sessions. She wanted to tell her story and be confirmed in it without discovering an enlarged world of meaning that would be unfamiliar and frightening. The substance of her experience cast a shadow that was not to be penetrated at this time in Wanda's life.

The story that Wanda related to me is not detailed, but there are some important clues for understanding her feelings at the time of the interviews. More importantly for this study, the sense of stalemate in life was not unique to Wanda and presents a challenge to a contemporary ministry. Wanda was active in the church through childhood and adolescence, but as an adult she felt that the church was artificial even though she was fairly regular in her attendance. The important transformations in her life were only peripherally related to the church and, although her sense of loss might have been weighted with religious meaning, she did not experience it this way. She believed that "way down deep it [the church] must be needed," but she had no immediate feeling of its importance. In Wanda's experience the church did not attend to the vision of a new reality that could challenge satisfaction with the shallow talk and conventional values of her childhood training.

Wanda reported very few memories of her primary school years. Her teachers liked her, and although she was shy she got along well with friends. She was close to her mother and even referred to her now as her "security blanket" during those early school years. She felt very plain as a child but enjoyed performing in class in front of her schoolmates. She wanted to be noticed. Her general feeling was that those were good years.

The strongest memory from Wanda's school years was an event that actually occurred at the onset of adolescence when she was thirteen years old. She had worn her hair in pigtails until this time when her mother decided to have Wanda's hair cut shorter. Wanda said that after her haircut everyone noticed her, and she was frightened by this new popularity that lasted through high school. It bothered her that she could not fulfill the expectations that were associated with popularity. She said that she was frightened because she didn't have much to say, and the haircut expanded her public arena. She was confused by this new sense of identity and felt inadequate.

Wanda interpreted her anxiety as an expression of shyness, but this explanation was not convincing for several reasons. First, she felt external support and affirmation. Her friends did not express disappointment or reinforce the feelings of inadequacy. Wanda was a pretty girl and this contributed to her teenage popularity. Her insecurity was more deeply rooted and lasted beyond the first blush of shyness at being noticed by schoolmates. Secondly, and more importantly, it was the train of associations that followed her recollection of the haircut that suggested a deeper source for the anxiety. She quickly related a series of dreams and fears that did not occur when she was thirteen but were juxtaposed in her thinking with the memory of the haircut.

Wanda was very concerned with being pretty, and her mother would tell her "pretty is as pretty does." This statement did not coincide with vague expectations that she associated with her popularity, and she was confused. In fact, she never articulated what these expectations were demanding of her. My only clues were the present chain of associated memories from early childhood and adult life. She was worried about tramps being in her house and was particularly frightened of the coal bin in the basement. She then related three dream fragments. The first was from childhood. Her house was on fire. This image was exciting to her. The only other time that she mentioned "fire" was when she told me a week later that "Mother was cold sexually. Daddy was on fire." The other fragments were from adult life. In the first she was pursued by a gorilla, which would hug her. In the second she was alone in her house and someone was coming after her.

These dream fragments suggest that the source of Wanda's anxiety was the inarticulate consciousness of internal desires that would threaten the stability of surface experience if they were expressed. The repressed desires were both libidinal and aggressive, but over the years the aggressive desires found a voice in family strife.

The libidinal feelings have not found a conscious voice in Wanda's world. Sexuality and spirituality were components of the self that could not be developed without threatening Wanda's provisional adjustment to her mother's values and conventional definition of the family. When Wanda was a teenager, she told her best girl friend that she really wanted to be an actress or go to modeling school. She then warned her not to tell anyone because she didn't want her mother to know this private fantasy. "She wouldn't want me to live that kind of life. The way I saw actors and actresses hugging and kissing wasn't done in my home. I saw it as unacceptable." Not only was it not acceptable, but Wanda was not able to understand her feelings.

Wanda approached her mother during adolescence with questions about the world of emotions and sexuality. These questions were never fully articulated because her mother would respond that "we don't talk about those kinds of things." It was Wanda's recollection that "those kinds of things" referred to everything that was important. The suppression of talk skewed the presentation of the imaginal world. The neighborhood of immediate experience was also increasingly narrowed. Her mother taught her that every touch was a sexual move to be feared. The eclipse of the imaginal world by the denial of language and the narrowing of the experiential world through suspicion and distrust left Wanda in a shallow world of convention and conformity. The unconscious needs for intimacy and depth continued as a fire in the basement of her psychic house. She was afraid of the tramp in her house but was pursued by this stranger that was also herself. The more these contents pressed for recognition the more she would say, "I am a controlled person. I keep myself in check. I want to remain in check."

The awareness of holding herself in check, according to her account, was not a recent achievement of understanding. The discrepancy between outward social acceptance and inner feelings continued through high school into the first two years of college. Although she was popular with other students, she felt inadequate and was afraid of being "found out" by her friends. Her feelings of inadequacy referred to the felt inability to integrate inner feelings and desires with the idealization of her self-image. Not only was she afraid of being found out by her friends, but she was also afraid of confronting the root of fantasy in herself. Her mother could no longer guarantee that the narrow world that she had fashioned, and which Wanda had accepted, was the real world of feeling and experience.

Wanda resolved the threat of an enlarging world of experience and freedom by entering into marriage. In Wanda's recollection of her engagement, her choice of a husband served two functions. Her fiancé was extroverted and enthusiastic about the broad range of life, and she was delighted and overwhelmed that someone like this could find her interesting. She felt that she could live through her husband. Even more important to her was the feeling that because her fiancé had deep religious convictions, he could be trusted not to fan the fire within her or open the door for the tramp in her psychic house. She said, "He was a Christian. I could rely on him. Marriage is submission to your husband." She thought that she could submit to this man without threatening the stability of her psychic house; and that, because he was outgoing, her needs for intimate human relationships could be satisfied through proxy. This sense of resolution lasted for about two years.

Wanda had little that she was willing to report about the next twenty years in her life. The desired redemption of the whole self through the achievements of her husband did not occur. She had ambivalent feelings about these years as a wife and mother. After the first two years of marriage she became conscious of an inability to fantasize. Reality was swallowed in a literalism of immediate experiences. There was no way to lift the drama of everydayness into a larger context of meaning. She had been denied the language to talk about what was real and important in life. She was afraid to respond to the multiplicity of internal feelings. A progressive homogenization of experience occurred as emotions were suspended in a psychological epoché. It would be naive to think that nothing of significance happened during these twenty years. However, important experiences were not integrated into a narrative affirmation of meaning. Important events were privileged episodes that were points of reference along a temporal continuum that did not tell the tales of their own becoming. The birth of children, major geographical moves, the growth of children and the rhythmic alternation of marital happiness and disappointment were experienced as interruptions and not as achievements of consciousness. Wanda described the experiences of this period of her life as a burden that she had to bear with courage and fortitude. She said, "I tried to please. I was in people's way. I was a doormat to be walked on."

Wanda thought that she was beginning to feel hope. She felt free to express her anger. She told her husband, "I don't have to take this crap anymore." Her anger constellated around a series of inverse insights. She knew how she did not want to live her life in the future but was not ready to translate these insights into an understanding of what she did want to do. The freedom to say no was itself experienced as an achievement. The withdrawal of consent from established family patterns had the impact of a question. The vague sense of hope was attendant to the flickering consciousness nourished by the shallow contrasts created by the inverse insights.

It was time in our working sessions to ask about the meaning of the inverse insights and better appraise the fragmented odyssey of Wanda's soul. Wanda wanted to terminate the interviews. There was to be no conscious appropriation of meaning, no homecoming, at this time. I accepted her decision with the request that I could talk with her again within the following year.

I interviewed her one year later. She had consolidated the feelings that were manifested at the end of our working sessions. She said, "I want to hang on to what I have." Wanda felt better about herself and no longer angry at her husband. In fact, she now claimed that her husband was her security. She thought that things were better because she was receiving medication for a past vitamin deficiency. The imaginal world had become safely contained. "I don't feel the fire anymore. For some reason I am at peace with myself." She explained, "My life has meaning in its own little niche." Her outreach into the world was now going to be through her children. Her children's lives would be the vessel for imagination, and she could remain in check. She re-affirmed her desire to constrict her own experience. "My stability and security is to keep myself in check. It is the only way that I can live."

Wanda extinguished the internal fire and alienated herself from the imaginal world so that she could feel at rest. The inability to thematize and articulate anything that was real and important had led to a silence interrupted only by occasional expressions of anger and frustration. The repression of language and understanding that began at home was not challenged but encouraged by the conservative voice of the church in her experience. The multiple voices of symbolism remained unconscious so that interpretation was always on one level. The mobility between levels of symbolic meaning was experienced as a fragmentation of life. The movement through the symbolic function was unconscious and was a movement from the restlessness of a deeper level to surface meanings. Wanda became locked in a literalism that was subjectively satisfied by objective interpretations of vitamin deficiencies or other physical dysfunctions.

We learn from the portrait of Wanda that ministry can enter into a complicity of denial in which the deeper voices of the symbolic function are gradually silenced. The failure first occurred in childhood and adolescence when there was no acceptance of the givenness of experience. "We don't talk about those kinds of things." Secondly, there was no invitation to share in a profound vision of what is real and important. The gospel was not proclaimed so that it was a challenge to literalistic reductions of meaning. Thirdly, the mobility through the symbolic voice was used to bring experience to the surface. That is, the mediation of meaning was directed toward maintaining a conventional opinion on the surface of experience rather than encouraging an experiment with the depths of life. It would now be difficult to open the meaning of theological symbolism because of the fear of opening symbols that would render Wanda's psychological adjustments indeterminate.

Part III

CONCLUSION

Chapter Five

THE MINISTRY AND THE CONTEMPORARY CHURCH

Re-visioning the task of the ministry is correlated with alterations in the practical concept of the church. The church should be conceived in such a way that it can contain the processes of ministry. The limits of the empirical church are often functionally expanded and sometimes even narrowed by the historical character of the life of the community of faith. Although the doctrine of the church is deeply rooted in the theological witness of the community, the image of the church is more frequently shaped by the quality of community life.

Creation, Christology, and eschatology must all be woven into the fabric of theological formulations defining the reality of the church.[1] Theology has spoken of the church as a mystery, the body of Christ, and as an eschatological reality. The integrity of this mystery has been protected by maintaining some expression of the distinction between the visible and the invisible church. This distinction placed the reality of the church beyond the measure of sociological analysis. The visible quality of life together always stands under a judgment of hope and promise. Thus, the visible church can at best be the assemblage of a pilgrim people that attend to an invisible meaning. Theology calls us forth to take account of invisible meaning when we stumble over the common weaknesses

---

[1]John Macquarrie, *Principles of Christian Theology*, 2nd edition (New York: Charles Scribner's Sons, 1977), p. 386.

of the empirical church. In fact, the quality of our life together is deepened by understanding or standing under the claims of the invisible church. We always remain underway. Theological formulations call our attention to this quality of experience.

The distinction between the visible and invisible church must be integrated into the life and work of the visible church if it is to be meaningful. The distinction is not an escape from secular judgment but is a confession that surface interpretations of experience do not adequately express what we have experienced as real and important. It is a claim made upon our own understanding, and re-visioning the task of ministry as practical hermeneutics is a response to this claim. A minister functions within the visible church by attending to that which is invisible. Of course, we can attend to what is invisible only by starting with what is visible. For example, we tell a story in order to find a story. The invisible delivers its message through the visible. Hermeneutics loosens the surface of experience so that we can look with-in and take account of what is newly visible. That which is in-visible adds to the meaning of our experience and alters the quality of life.

Contemporary church life should be analyzed. It needs to be loosened throughout. We cannot know the in-visible church without inward thinking and downward thinking. The upward and outward thrust of many liturgical reforms expresses an important moment in the shared life of the church, but the reforms cannot be substituted for the whole of life together without a loss of meaning. The theology of glory is internally related to the theology of the cross. Joyful celebrations with bells and banners stand in a configuration with Golgotha, scorning laughter, bleeding wounds, sour sop, and betrayal.[2] Preaching, teaching, and counseling can all contribute to the inward thinking of the community. Inward thinking and outward commitment involve each other. Both concepts are overdetermined in the organic unity of experience. One of the tasks of ministry is to disclose this coincidence of meaning and merge the vocations of priest and prophet. The meaning of the visible church swells with the growth of ministerial functions. The meaning of the in-visible church is increasingly valued.

The first task of the ministry is to accept the givenness of experience. We can challenge the adequacy of experience but we cannot depart from it if we are to possess our own story. The "mighty acts of God" are meaningless unless they resonate on some level with what we have experienced to be real and important.

The acceptance of experience requires interpretation. Experience is often disguised and masked so that we cannot easily

[2]Cf. James Hillman, *Re-Visioning Psychology* (New York: Harper & Row, 1975), p. 95.

assess the meaning of our beginning in the middle. We are not always willing to recognize that we are animals of instinct and desire. It is the lesson of psychoanalysis that we compromise with societal values by realizing our desires through disguise, regression, and symbolization.[3] It is not enough to proclaim acceptance and the forgiveness of sins. We first must come to an understanding of what we mean by sin on the first level of experience. Then we must see through the manifest content of experience to its hidden voices before the words of acceptance have any real depth. A shallow understanding of the human condition is not a realistic beginning. We perpetuate a charade if the moment of confession is not also an unmasking of comfortable disguises that easily embrace the subtle transgressions of sublimated desires. We see this type of unmasking in the teachings of Jesus as well as in psychoanalytic interpretation. For example, it is hard to escape the power of the following New Testament verses from Matthew: "You have heard that it was said to the men of old, 'You shall not kill; and whoever kills shall be liable to judgment.' But I say to you that every one who is angry with his brother shall be liable to judgment" (Matt. 5:21,22) or "You have heard that it was said, 'You shall not commit adultery.' But I say to you that every one who looks at a woman lustfully has already committed adultery with her in his heart" (Matt. 5:27,28). It is here that we begin in the middle. The catalogue of common defenses must be seen for what they are.

To accept the givenness of experience requires interpretation. The collection of events and ideas that constitute the middle of experience are selected from the complex whole of life. Certain experiences press symptomatically for special recognition and are reinforced by physical complaints or amplified emotions. Other experiences are noticeable because of their suspicious isolation or dislocation. Still other experiences must be brought into conscious awareness by selectively attending to their quiet voices. Simple collection is the most basic form of interpretation.

Accepting the givenness of experience is more than simple collection. Masking and disguise can distort our sense of beginning in the middle. The phenomenon of masking implies the existence of hidden or repressed meanings in the givenness of experience. To recognize a mask is also to know that there is a face hidden behind the mask. The face as well as the mask constitute the meaning of experience. Even if we do not recognize the face, we must give a place for its meaning in our act of acceptance. For example, if we only accept the mask of piety that covers the face of an adulterer of

---

[3]Paul Ricoeur, *Freud and Philosophy: An Essay on Interpretation* (New Haven: Yale University Press, 1970), p. 162.

the heart, the word of acceptance is shallow and contributes to a complicity of denial. There is no real freedom to dream the story onward if we do not first recognize the story that is being told.

Beginning in the middle of experience makes a claim upon the role of the church. The church must be open to prostitutes and tax collectors even when they appear behind the pious masks of civic virtue. The church must learn to live in "bad company" and be able to thematize and articulate the shadow side of human nature.[4] Otherwise, its myths are reduced to fables, and the words of acceptance are diminished to saccharine sentimentalities that offer no real hope or understanding. Primary collection is a priestly caring for the wholeness of experience and a prophetic unmasking that allows us to value what is in-visible.

The second task on the revised agenda for the ministry is invitation. This task also makes a claim on our understanding of the role of the church. Invitation is usually associated with a preaching ministry; but it is also connected with liturgy, teaching, and counseling. Invitation is intimately connected with the interpretation of experience. The significance of acceptance is deepened by an invitation to participate in a more satisfying vision of what is real and important. It is both a proclamation and a witness to the meaning of conversion. In the context of preaching and proclamation, invitation often occurs by drawing attention to paradigmatic conversion stories in the religious traditions of a community. When Raden Djaka Sahid met Sunan Bonang, his vision of what was real and important was radically altered. The story that he was carrying forward was pale and meaningless in the face of Sunan Bonang's access to the power of Allah. The transformation of Saul into Paul and the callings of Peter, James, and John all tell the tale of a deepening vision of reality that creates discontent with shallow understanding and one-dimensional living.

Invitation can also be a personal confession or witness to the presence of a story that is in-visible. The confession is sometimes itself a story of descent that points to new possibilities for interpretation but is not the interpretation. Sometimes it is the interpretation or telling of the new story. Invitation as confession is an acknowledgment of the commonality of human possibilities even in the particularity of individual life. Personal confirmation in the articulation of deeper levels of narrative meaning is implicitly an invitation to others to share in downward thinking. Our stories resonate with each other on the deepest levels. This is the lure and power of a "case study" or "Wednesday night" prayer and testimony service. Someone has been turned around, and the public

[4]Cf. Adolf Holl, *Jesus in Bad Company* (New York: Holt, Rinehart and Winston, 1972).

acknowledgment of conversion alters the collective consciousness of what is possible.

Conversion is not always experienced as being turned around. Sometimes it is a more accurate description to say that we have been turned upside down. What belonged in the dark spaces of experience is advancing into the light. The imagination is restored to its seriousness and magnitude in the flux of life. Invitation suggests restoration, recovery, discovery, and expansion. A decision is inevitable. Are we going to respond to the possibility for the determination of new meanings in the ordinary configurations of experience? Invitation implies a question addressed to life.

The force of questioning first appears negative. Familiar patterns of adaptation are rendered indeterminate by the shifting context for interpretation. However, the destruction of settled forms is also a restoration of meaning. Questioning embraces meaning in a new context, on a deeper level of interpretation, or under an expanded horizon. If we account for the overdetermination of meaning in symbolic expressions, any single pattern of interpretation or adaptation lacks closure. Suddenly the solid surface becomes liquified. We struggle to stay afloat amidst a fluid surplus of meaning. For example, this is evident where common sense is confounded by the parabolic teachings of Jesus or the specter of Dionysian ecstasy. In most of the paradigmatic expressions of transformation in religious and mythological traditions, we sense that loosening our grip on what we have already achieved is a risky action.

A ministry that focuses attention on symbolic thinking must be prepared to accept this risk. The prophetic unmasking in the ministry of acceptance is a preparation of the parishioner to meet this risk. That is, we are willing to accept risk only when we realize that not to accept the risk that accompanies downward thinking is to be trapped in an unsatisfactory compromise with surface experience. The minister must not only prepare others but also be prepared to accept the dissolution in the parishioner's life. This is part of an emergent story. Depth requires a tenacious grip on the whole of experience including extreme expressions such as the oblivion of despair and hopelessness. There must be patience with confusion and obscured vision. Hasty affirmations of meaning betray the depth that is sought by abbreviating the seasons of life with their rich display of possibilities. When an invitation is issued, a time and place must be prepared for its acceptance. This is one of the radical functions of the church in a secular society.

Very simply, the church is a place to wait and experience. Liturgy and theology constellate archetypal situations, provide times, and make spaces for transformations in hurried lives.

Initiation, descent, sacrifice, and abandonment are some of the familiar religio-psychological themes symbolically valenced and ritually enacted in the church's memory that provide a language for downward thinking.[5] By attending to its own witness the church is naturally a place for the deepening of consciousness. It is ironic that, in a time when it has desperately sought a relevant voice in secular life, one of the church's most relevant and radical functions is that it can secure a time and place for transformation through the conservation of its inheritance. However, the church endangers the realization of this important function if it confuses literalism with the conservation of meaning. Symbolic thinking is an opening and not a closure. This acknowledgment leads to the third task in practical hermeneutics—the mediation of meaning.

An interpretive ministry contributes to the privilege of consciousness by drawing symbols and mythological ideas from history and tradition that establish the necessary contrasts for the deepening of experience. That is, a new consciousness is possible when everyday experience is contrasted against an archetypal background. Not only do we account for religious and mythological meanings; but, more importantly, everyday experience becomes the carrier of new meaning. We experience the world differently. We are no longer trapped in blind immediacy or shallow literalism.

The care for traditional symbols and mythology provides a language for the restoration of the imagination and subsequent mediation of meaning. It becomes possible to think mythologically and fantasize personal symbols and symptoms forward to the story they imply. The vaguely apprehended context of possibilities that surround the concretization of experience becomes valenced for conscious appreciation with the complexification of contrast at the ground of consciousness. The surface of experience remains significant in itself, but surface level interpretations do not exhaust the totality of meaning. For example, in the story of James L. social action was a meaningful task; but we had to refer to a mythic level of interpretation before we could assess its significance and satisfaction in his life. The mediation of meaning is a constructive theological task at the heart of the ministry. It is a unique responsibility for which there are no secular substitutes. Psychologizing intersects theology when the symbol gives rise to thought.

The intersection of interpretive patterns in the multivalence of the symbol gives mobility for the mediation of meaning. We can enter the symbol on a shallow level of immediate presentation and

---

[5]Cf. James Hillman, *Loose Ends: Primary Papers in Archetypal Psychology* (Zurich: Spring Publications, 1975), pp. 185–86.

journey to deeper levels of meaning. This is the expansive function of practical hermeneutics and the significance of the call for the mediation of meaning. This is, however, a danger implicit in the mobility of symbolic thinking. The symbols are double-vectored. We can move through them in either direction. If we resist the expansion of consciousness, the encounter with depth symbols in life crises can be depotentiated by moving through the symbol to the surface. The symbol is then literalized in a one-dimensional interpretation. Experience is shut down in all of its complementary modes. Psychological and theological closure imply each other. This is particularly troublesome in practical parish life. Preaching that aims at opening the symbolic voice of theological understanding will also open psychological symbols. The well-intentioned commitment to theological understanding can be undermined by inappropriate psychological timing. The intersection of private and traditional uses of religious language in the story of Catherine T. illustrates this interdependence of interpretive frameworks. The mediation of meaning must be prepared for psychologically and theologically or there will be hidden resistances.

Acceptance, invitation, and the mediation of meaning contribute to the overinterpretation that might be considered a fourth movement in a revised agenda for the ministry. However, they are all movements within the process of re-collection or overinterpretation. Acceptance and invitation are ways of descent into the depth of psyche. The mediation of meaning supplies the religio-mythological background for the retelling of a story. There is already an active engagement in the creation of a collaborative fiction.

The conscious entertainment of archetypal patterns and religious themes is an interpretive experiment in imaginal thinking. The church itself becomes an experimental vessel for human transformation and the intensification of consciousness. The articulation of an imaginal background to thinking is at the same time an appropriation of the actual realization of individual existence. That is, the consciousness of actuality emerges when a contrast has been established against a background of imaginal possibilities. There is a reciprocity in the consciousness that attends archetypal and personal storytelling. On one hand, personal experience is woven into the texture of mythological themes and is illuminated by those themes. On the other hand, mythology is valenced for personal life, concretized, and weighted with an existential confirmation of meaning.

Re-collection is a process and requires an ongoing collaboration. It is a continual attending to the vision of reality that was a constitutive element in the meaning of conversion. The theological task of "naming the whirlwind" is a psychological wrestling with angels. It is an arduous and downward journey. If we stay with the task, we might be blessed with a new name. That is, we might recognize ourselves in a story that is real and important.

INDEX